First World War
and Army of Occupation
War Diary
France, Belgium and Germany

18 DIVISION
Headquarters, Branches and Services
Royal Army Ordnance Corps
Assistant Director Ordnance Services
21 July 1915 - 28 February 1919

WO95/2023/2

The Naval & Military Press Ltd
www.nmarchive.com
Published in association with The National Archives

Published by

The Naval & Military Press Ltd

Unit 10 Ridgewood Industrial Park,

Uckfield, East Sussex,

TN22 5QE England

Tel: +44 (0) 1825 749494

www.naval-military-press.com

www.nmarchive.com

This diary has been reprinted in facsimile from the original. Any imperfections are inevitably reproduced and the quality may fall short of modern type and cartographic standards.

© **Crown Copyright**
Images reproduced by permission of The National Archives, London, England, 2015.

Contents

Document type	Place/Title	Date From	Date To
Heading	WO95/2023/2		
Heading	18th Division A.D.O.S. Jly 1915-Feb 1919		
Heading	18th Division Headquarters 18th Div: D.A.D.O.S. Vol: I Jly & Aug 15		
Heading	War Diary of D.A.D.O.S. 18th Division From 21st July 1915 To 31st August 1915 Volume 1		
War Diary	Boulongne	21/07/1915	21/07/1915
War Diary	St. Omer	22/07/1915	22/07/1915
War Diary	Flesselles	24/07/1915	07/08/1915
War Diary	Montigny	08/08/1915	19/08/1915
War Diary	Heilly	19/08/1915	31/08/1915
Heading	18th Division 18th Division D.A.D.O.S. Vol II Sept 15		
Heading	War Diary of D.A.D.O.S. 18th Division From 1st September 1915 To 30th September 1915		
War Diary	Heilly	01/09/1915	30/09/1915
Heading	18th Division H.Q. 18th Div: D.A.D.O.S. Vol 3 Oct 15		
Heading	War Diary of D A D O S 18th Div. From 1st October 1915 To 31st October 1915		
War Diary	Heilly	01/10/1915	28/10/1915
Heading	18th Div. D.A.D.S.O. Vol. 4 121/7635 Nov 15		
Heading	War Diary of D.A.D.O.S. 18th Division From 1st November 1915 To 30th November 1915		
War Diary	Heilly	06/11/1915	30/11/1915
Heading	D.A.D.S.O. 18th Div. Vol 5 Dec		
Heading	War Diary of D.A.D.S.O. 18th Division from 1st Dec. 1915 to 31st December 1915		
War Diary	Heilly	01/12/1915	31/12/1915
Heading	War Diary of D.A.D.O.S. 18th Division from 1st Jan 1916 to 31st January 1916 Vol VI		
War Diary	Heilly	01/01/1916	31/01/1916
Heading	D.A.D.O.S. 18th Division Vol VII 18 Div		
Heading	War Diary of D.A.D.O.S. 18th Div For Month of February 1916		
War Diary	Heilly	01/02/1916	05/02/1916
War Diary	Ribemont	06/02/1916	29/02/1916
Heading	War Diary of D.A.D.O.S. 18th Division From 1st March16 To 31st March 16		
War Diary	Ribemont	01/03/1916	05/03/1916
War Diary	Montigny	06/03/1916	19/03/1916
War Diary	Etinehem	20/03/1916	30/04/1916
Heading	War Diary of D.A.D.O.S. 18th Division For March Of May 1915 Vol 10		
War Diary	Etinehem	01/05/1916	04/05/1916
War Diary	Ailly Sur Somme	05/05/1916	31/05/1916
Heading	War Diary For The Month of June 16 Vol 12		
War Diary	Ailly Sur Somme	01/06/1916	17/06/1916
War Diary	Corbie	18/06/1916	30/06/1916
Heading	D.A.D.O.S. 18th Division 18 Vol 12		
Heading	War Diary of D.A.D.O.S. 18th Div: For The Month Of July 1916		

War Diary	Corbie	01/07/1916	22/07/1916
War Diary	Hallencourt	23/07/1916	23/07/1916
War Diary	Reniscure	24/07/1916	31/07/1916
Heading	War Diary of D.A.D.O.S. 18 Div: For The Month of August 16		
War Diary	Reniscure	01/08/1916	02/08/1916
War Diary	Croix Du Bac	03/08/1916	23/08/1916
War Diary	Bailleul	24/08/1916	24/08/1916
War Diary	Roellecourt	25/08/1916	08/09/1916
War Diary	Doullens	09/09/1916	10/09/1916
War Diary	Achicourt	11/09/1916	30/09/1916
War Diary	Hedauville	01/10/1916	06/10/1916
War Diary	Bernaville	07/10/1916	16/10/1916
War Diary	Albert	17/10/1916	21/11/1916
War Diary	Buigny St Maclou	22/11/1916	30/11/1916
Heading	War Diary of D.A.D.O.S. 18th Div. From 1 To 31 December 1916 Vol 17		
War Diary	Buigny St Maclou	01/12/1916	15/01/1917
War Diary	Hedauville	15/01/1917	28/02/1917
War Diary	Bouzincourt	01/03/1917	23/03/1917
War Diary	Steenbecque	26/03/1917	29/03/1917
Heading	18 D.W.A		
War Diary	Steenbecque	01/04/1917	15/04/1917
War Diary	Labeuvriere	22/04/1917	29/04/1917
War Diary	Dainville	28/04/1917	28/04/1917
Heading	18 D.W.A.		
War Diary	Dainville	01/05/1917	05/05/1917
War Diary	Le Chal Maigre	14/05/1917	15/05/1917
War Diary	Boisleux Au Mont	22/05/1917	31/05/1917
War Diary	Couin	01/07/1917	04/07/1917
War Diary	Steenvorde	06/07/1917	06/07/1917
War Diary	Renninghelst	07/07/1917	15/08/1917
War Diary	Lederzeele	17/08/1917	01/09/1917
War Diary	Esquelbec	03/09/1917	23/09/1917
War Diary	Vogeltje	26/09/1917	29/09/1917
Miscellaneous	Messages And Signals.		
Miscellaneous	A Form Messages And Signals.		
War Diary	Vogeltje	02/10/1917	31/10/1917
War Diary	Elverdinghe	15/11/1917	31/12/1917
War Diary	Rousbrugge	01/01/1918	01/01/1918
War Diary	Elverdinghe	03/01/1918	29/01/1918
War Diary	Rousbrugge	01/02/1918	07/02/1918
War Diary	Saleux	08/02/1918	28/02/1918
War Diary	Villequier Aumont	04/03/1918	24/03/1918
War Diary	Baboeuf	24/03/1918	24/03/1918
War Diary	Theiscourt	25/03/1918	25/03/1918
War Diary	Estree St Denis	26/03/1918	26/03/1918
War Diary	Audignicourt	27/03/1918	27/03/1918
War Diary	Estree St Denis	28/03/1918	28/03/1918
War Diary	Berneuil	29/03/1918	29/03/1918
War Diary	Compieful	29/03/1918	29/03/1918
War Diary	Hebecourt	30/03/1918	30/03/1918
War Diary	St Sauflieu	30/03/1918	04/04/1918
War Diary	Saleux	05/04/1918	26/04/1918
War Diary	Cavillon	27/04/1918	22/05/1918
War Diary	Mollens Au Bois	23/05/1918	30/06/1918

Miscellaneous	18th Division 17	16/08/1918	16/08/1918
Miscellaneous	A Form Messages And Signals.		
War Diary	Mollens Au Bois	01/07/1918	12/07/1918
War Diary	Cavillon	13/07/1918	31/07/1918
War Diary	Contay	18/08/1918	24/08/1918
War Diary	Warloy	25/08/1918	25/08/1918
War Diary	Ribemont	26/08/1918	31/08/1918
War Diary	St Gratien	01/08/1918	11/08/1918
War Diary	Contay	12/08/1918	17/08/1918
War Diary	Ribemont Fricourt	01/09/1918	15/09/1918
War Diary	Nurlu	16/09/1918	24/09/1918
War Diary	Combles	25/09/1918	27/09/1918
War Diary	Nurlu	28/09/1918	30/09/1918
Miscellaneous	18 Div A	08/11/1918	08/11/1918
Miscellaneous	Instant And Onwards. Revised Orders Are Being Reception Camps.	27/10/1918	27/10/1918
War Diary	Nurlu	01/10/1918	31/10/1918
War Diary	Le Cateau	01/11/1918	26/11/1918
War Diary	Serain Ligny	01/12/1918	31/12/1918
Heading	18 Div A	28/02/1919	28/02/1919
War Diary	Ligny	01/02/1919	28/02/1919

WO 95/2023 (2)

18TH DIVISION

A. D. O. S.

JLY 1915-FEB 1919

121/6753

18th Division

Headquarters 18th Div:
84.8.05
Vol. I
July & Aug 15

Army Form C. 2118

Confidential

WAR DIARY
or
~~INTELLIGENCE SUMMARY~~

(Erase heading not required.)

Instructions regarding War Diaries and Intelligence Summaries are contained in F. S. Regs., Part II. and the Staff Manual respectively. Title Pages will be prepared in manuscript.

Place	Date	Hour	Summary of Events and Information	Remarks and references to Appendices
				3

[Stamp: A.B.S OFFICE AT THE BASE / 12 SEP 1915 / A.O.C. SECTION]

Confidential

WAR DIARY

of

D.A.D.O.S 18th DIVISION

From 21st July 1915 To 31st August 1915

Volume 1

1875 W¹ W 593/826 1,000,000 4/15 J.B.C. & A. A.D.S.S./Forms/C. 2118

Army Form C. 2118

WAR DIARY
or
INTELLIGENCE SUMMARY
(Erase heading not required.)

Instructions regarding War Diaries and Intelligence Summaries are contained in F.S. Regs., Part II. and the Staff Manual respectively. Title Pages will be prepared in manuscript.

Place	Date	Hour	Summary of Events and Information	Remarks and references to Appendices
BOULOGNE	21/7/15		Arrived with advance part, and stayed the night	A.9
ST OMER	22/7/15		Carried from BOULOGNE to G.H.Q and went with General Questelme with D.A.D.O.S. 3rd Army.	A.9
FLESSELLES	24/7/15		Arrived at Divisional Head Quarters. Owing to Divisional Area to be occupied fixed it necessary to establish from existing points. Visited Corps and Army Head Quarters.	A.9
— do —	25/7/15		Refilling points for Area are, FLESSELLES, MOLLIEN au BON, TALMAS and RAMPONNET.	A.9
— do —	26/7/15		Conferred with A.A. & Q.M.G. on general procedure.	A.9
— do —	27/7/15		Divisional Head Quarters arrived - Railhead fixed at ST ROCH 8 miles from Head Quarters.	A.9
— do —	28/7/15 29/7/15		Units of Division arriving	A.9

4

WAR DIARY
or
INTELLIGENCE SUMMARY

Army Form C. 2118

Place	Date	Hour	Summary of Events and Information	Remarks and references to Appendices
PITTSBURG	30/7		Completion of arrival of Division – Instructed Refugee Warned officers as to procedure adopted & arranged them to Train Companies A.S.C. as being more convenient for refilling point.	A.F.
do	31/7		Visited Area in connection with Reserve lorries Park Supply Column stores at same time as supplies found that supply wagons Lorries were rather very little from us, as their wagons were well loaded. Supplies in the Case of both came a second journey would have to be made.	A.Q.
do	1/8/15		It certainly to not an easy matter breakdown up stores in a Railway Truck to send out to fix Refilling points but as early move is contemplated, check to time provisions visited by D.D.O.S.	A.Q.
do	2/8/15		On 18th Brigade, as Howitzer Battery, a R.E. Sig. Company and on Infantry Brigade leave for inundation visit 5th Division – 9 Attached Brigade Warrant Officer & his 2 men to WARLOY to look after them – Railhead moved to MERICOURT.	A.Q.

LARGE.

WAR DIARY

Army Form C. 2118

Place	Date	Hour	Summary of Events and Information	Remarks and references to Appendices
FRESNES	3/7/15		One Officer R.F.A., 1 Transport Officer attached for instruction to 5th Brigade. Brigade warrant officer at WARLOY to look after Brigade.	A.G.
do	4/7/15		Visit from D.D.O.S. 3rd Army appeared satisfied.	A.G.
do	5/7/15		Machine guns arrived to complete to 4 per Battalion. An units have been continually employed about billets and erect shelters to take cover.	A.G.
do	6/7/15		The new Railhead a much more suitable place. Everything going on satisfactorily.	A.G.
do	7/7/15		Visited MONTIGNY on new Divisional Head Qrs. Located a Central refilling point - have arranged for all three Brigades to draw their detailed units there, so as to WARLOY Ry lorry stuff, all other units draw from refilling point.	A.G.
MONTIGNY	8/7/15		Divisional Hd Qrs shifted today, much nearer Railhead, which is more satisfactory. 55th Infantry Brigade with attached for instruction to 5th Division. Received a refilling point at TR VILLE SUR LANE and detached Brigade warrant officer there, who also looks over the Batteries attached.	A.G.

6

WAR DIARY or INTELLIGENCE SUMMARY

Army Form C. 2118

Place	Date	Hour	Summary of Events and Information	Remarks and references to Appendices
MONTIGNY	9/7		Went round new Area, various units all appear settled with very slow one coming along. Any weak are [far] part — Pioneer battalion detailed to 51st Division for instruction —	A.9
"	10/7		Conferred with O i/c Section of Landry. On being shewn that under 51st Div. Ambulance demanded 1000 changes of underclothing in reserve —	A.9
			Machine gun ammn completing all battalions to full strength —	A.9
"	11/7		Ordinary routine	
"	12/7		One 4.5" reported burst, investigation before taking action — am awaiting I.O.M.'s report —	A.9
"	13/7		18 pr. 4"c" gun turns out to be a 18 pr. gun. Badly [fired?] quite beyond repair - demands in to replace - to the need for immediate action Rec. reports before wiring off for guns to replace -	A.9

7

Place	Date	Hour	Summary of Events and Information	Remarks and references to Appendices
MONTIGNY	14/11		Visited by Major J. Baker DADOS. 3rd Army, who interviewed O.C. on question of workshops. It is desired all to commence the old style until we get into our billeting area, an ovens to so many trucks being detached to in such a scattered area no free furnace will be served.	A.G.
—	15/11		1.15 pm arrived to replace the burnt out 53rd Infantry Brigade with return from by battalions to the Division. Brigade Warrant Officer 54th Infantry Brigade fer feer first to report after them.	A/427 A.G. A.G.
—	16/11		Present system of main working satisfactory. Brigade R.F.A. rejoined Division.	
—	17/11		Went to AMIENS to purchase material for Rifle Grout Primus antenna owing to shortage of Eafour. Found a firm "CAPON" who is making samples are for POE to see. Cost 70 centimes.	A.G. A.G.

Army Form C. 2118

WAR DIARY
or
INTELLIGENCE SUMMARY

(Erase heading not required.)

Place	Date	Hour	Summary of Events and Information	Remarks and references to Appendices
MONTIGNY	18/4/15		Division under orders to move. Located a store at MERICOURT put south of Railhead for refilling from Ordre place for Rifle Covers —	a.9.
	19/4/15		Hd Qrs of Division shifted to HEILLY — trenches now in new area reconnoitred taking over part line of Trenches in the next two days —	a.9.
HEILLY	20/4/15		53rd Infantry Brigade relieved Divisional Gatherers & R.E. from in the Corner of the next two days.	a.9.
"	21/4/15		Visited 535 Infantry Brigade at BRAY in connection with reins of Stores arranged to send by Lorry to trucks as at billets.	a.9.
"	22/4/15		Road leading to BRAY having been shelled. Lorries	a.9.
"	23/4/15		13th Bde: will now divert them from refilling point BOIS DE TAILLES	a.9.

Army Form C. 2118

WAR DIARY
or
INTELLIGENCE SUMMARY
(Erase heading not required.)

Instructions regarding War Diaries and Intelligence Summaries are contained in F.S. Regs, Part II. and the Staff Manual respectively. Title Pages will be prepared in manuscript.

10

Place	Date	Hour	Summary of Events and Information	Remarks and references to Appendices
HEILLY	24/7/15		Everything working smoothly	
"	25/7/15		Consulted Q on question of workshops. Brigadiers orders for this view.	A.Q.
"	26/7/15			
"	27/7/15		D.D.M.S. 3rd Army visited Q in connection with formation of workshops - nothing yet definitely decided.	A.Q.
"	28/7/15		Visited TRUEX to create site for workshops. went with Q to Brigadier S.C. of Brigade in this connection.	A.Q.
"	29/7/15			A.Q.
"	30/7/15		Slow decision to open small ammunition dump. Arrangements made for them work to be carried out in A.O.D. Shed. This does not affect 53rd infantry Brigade and other units at BRAY.	A.Q.
"	31/7/15			A.Q.

12/6930.

18th Division

18th Division O.A. & O.S.
Vol II
Sept. 15

Army Form C. 2118

WAR DIARY
or
INTELLIGENCE SUMMARY
(Erase heading not required.)

Confidential

WAR DIARY
of
D.A.D.O.S. 18th Division
From 1st September 1915 To 30th September 1915

(Capt. A. Kulcher
R.A.O.D)

12

A.O.D. STORE AT THE BASE — 3 OCT 1915 — A.O.C. SECTION

Army Form C. 2118

WAR DIARY
or
INTELLIGENCE SUMMARY

(Erase heading not required.)

Place	Date	Hour	Summary of Events and Information	Remarks and references to Appendices
HELLY	1/7/15		Visited 13th Infantry Brigade HQrs at BRAY – found Certified with the way things were being carried on. RA Units still wanting spare parts for packs.	a.g.
do	2/7/15		Visited 2nd Army Head Qrs. Conference with DDOS on various subjects.	a.g.
do	3/7/15			a.g.
do	4/7/15			a.g.
do	5/7/15		Visited by DDOS 2nd Army – Everything working smoothly.	a.g.
do	6/7/15			a.g.
do	7/7/15			a.g.
do	8/7/15			a.g.

13

Army Form C. 2118

WAR DIARY
or
INTELLIGENCE SUMMARY

(Erase heading not required.)

Instructions regarding War Diaries and Intelligence Summaries are contained in F. S. Regs., Part II. and the Staff Manual respectively. Title Pages will be prepared in manuscript.

14

Place	Date	Hour	Summary of Events and Information	Remarks and references to Appendices
HEILLY	9/9		Everything normal meanwhile all ranks engaged with the usual store in connection with our move and in preparing for scheme	Q.3
"	10/9			Q.3
"	11/9			Q.3
"	12/9			Q.3
"	13/9			Q.3
"	14/9			Q.3
"	15/9			G.3
"	16/9		1st Infantry Brigade moved from BRAY and up near other Brigades. HQ now at ALBERT. This reminds collection of prisoners.	Q.3

1875 Wt. W593/826 1,000,000 4/15 J.B.C. & A. A.D.S.S./Forms/C. 2118.

Army Form C. 2118

WAR DIARY
or
INTELLIGENCE SUMMARY
(Erase heading not required.)

Instructions regarding War Diaries and Intelligence Summaries are contained in F. S. Regs., Part II. and the Staff Manual respectively. Title Pages will be prepared in manuscript.

Place	Date	Hour	Summary of Events and Information	Remarks and references to Appendices
HEILLY	9/11/15		Infantry Battalions sent billets shifted from RIBEMONT, MERICOURT & VILLE s/ANCRE, HEAULT, DERNACOURT, MORLANCOURT. Divisional Troops moved to RIBEMONT and MERICOURT.	
	14/11		Sent to O.C. Units nott nominate places from which	
			(heard) MERICOURT	
	19/11 20/11		Orders by AA QMG to stop storing in reserve coming up temporarily owing to a contemplated advance. Wires accordingly eaten half of P—ge trench, and from kilo. machine gun heads Technical Stores one a few other main items to await instructions for the present.	

15

WAR DIARY
or
INTELLIGENCE SUMMARY

(Erase heading not required.)

Army Form C. 2118

Instructions regarding War Diaries and Intelligence Summaries are contained in F. S. Regs., Part II. and the Staff Manual respectively. Title Pages will be prepared in manuscript.

16

Place	Date	Hour	Summary of Events and Information	Remarks and references to Appendices
HELLES	21/5		In the event of a move I am not ready. I have to store (over)	
-//-	22/5		1(Q) headquarters at the Flotilla and 146 Tents - In addition I have 20,000 more tents. Retents- bivouacs- awnings are being made which also effects all tents here from	a.a.
-//-	23/5		each canopy, which also effects all tents here from	a.a.
-//-	24/5		Body adjustment flag wanted some to war from 13000 3rd army.	a.a.
-//-	25/5			a.a.
-//-	26/5			a.a.

WAR DIARY or INTELLIGENCE SUMMARY

Army Form C. 2118

Place	Date	Hour	Summary of Events and Information	Remarks and references to Appendices
HEILLY	27/9			
-"-	28/9		Have received the experience of three for the time being.	O.C.
-"-	29/9		Stores coming along well except spare parts for 18/pr, 3" & 6" Howitzer and 6mm machine guns otherwise limits well satisfied.	O.C.
-"-	30/9		Visit from Major Baker Baron, 3rd Army. I viewed all a.a. buck once or more during the month even though all outstanding details.	O.C. A Salcher Capt 30/9 batter 18th Bgd.

17

18th Kurram

12/7517

H.D. 18th Sri: S.A. Vol.

Vol 3

Oct 15.

pros

18

Army Form C. 2118

WAR DIARY
or
INTELLIGENCE SUMMARY
(Erase heading not required.)

Instructions regarding War Diaries and Intelligence Summaries are contained in F. S. Regs., Part II. and the Staff Manual respectively. Title Pages will be prepared in manuscript.

19

Confidential

WAR DIARY
of
D.A.D.O.S 18th Divn
From 1st October 1915 To 31st October 1915

WAR DIARY or INTELLIGENCE SUMMARY

Army Form C. 2118

Place	Date	Hour	Summary of Events and Information	Remarks and references to Appendices
HEILLY	1/10/15		A line Railway establishment started in ALBERT. Enquires being made whether women can be obtained for washing the clothing. Enquiries sent as to understanding asked for —	A.Q.
-"-	2/10/15		Visited 53rd Infantry Brigade Head Qrs; in connection with Bostn. Staff Captain considers 1000 pairs shoes to feet in the Brigade, as [crossed out] in the event of an advance he [inaudible] of getting them up might be a number — I pointed out that supplies would come up to Railhead wherever we were, and as the question of Transport was involved he agreed with my views.	
-"-	3/10/15			A.Q.
-"-	4/10/15			A.Q.
-"-	5/10/15		Sufficient women labour found in ALBERT for Carnoy. Have allowance 1500 sets of Underclothing to about A.O.	A.Q.

20

Army Form C. 2118

WAR DIARY
or
INTELLIGENCE SUMMARY
(Erase heading not required.)

21

Place	Date	Hour	Summary of Events and Information	Remarks and references to Appendices
HEILLY	6/17			
"	7/17		Have arranged with OC 13th Casualty line of 3 ambulances from this trust for evacuation of sick. We have arranged for a system in RIBEMONT. Behaviour will still carry but their refugees unfortunately but stops living for refugees to	Q.9
"	8/17		R.A.M.C. and small huts. It is hoped to do about 300 pairs monthly.	Q.9
"	9/17			Q.9
"	10/17		Even machine run from some faith died refugees limits	Q.9
"	11/17		Continually heathering, had no supplies at Base.	Q.9

Army Form C. 2118

WAR DIARY
or
INTELLIGENCE SUMMARY

(Erase heading not required.)

Place	Date	Hour	Summary of Events and Information	Remarks and references to Appendices
HESDIN	12/10			
"	13/10		Nil to [?] 3rd Army	O.2
"	14/10			O.2
"	15/10			
"	16/10		On sick leave for the last two days. Have seen my Chief Clerk. Looked after everything most satisfactory. Everything going on well & supplies coming along with exception of meat bags of which there has been a shortage for the last two weeks.	
"	17/10		Visited BEAUQUESNE and Conferred with D.D.O.S. on various subjects —	O.2 O.2
"	18/10			O.2

22

Army Form C. 2118

WAR DIARY
or
INTELLIGENCE SUMMARY

(Erase heading not required.)

Instructions regarding War Diaries and Intelligence Summaries are contained in F. S. Regs., Part II. and the Staff Manual respectively. Title Pages will be prepared in manuscript.

Place	Date	Hour	Summary of Events and Information	Remarks and references to Appendices
HEILLY	19/10/15			A.2
-//-	20/10/15			A.2
-//-	21/10/15			A.2
-//-	22/10/15	Supplies coming up well, with exception of wax bags.		A.2
-//-	23/10/15	These are very short.		A.2
-//-	24/10/15			A.3
-//-	25/10/15			A.2
-//-	26/10/15			A.2

23

Place	Date	Hour	Summary of Events and Information	Remarks and references to Appendices
HEILLY	27/5		183rd Tunnelling Co RE & 253rd Tunnelling Co RE joined the Division, the latter only 50 strong. The preceding drafts of RE reinforcements to the 5th Railway being so far away, I am having to send for ordnance supplies.	
	28/5		here on to 107th Field Co: RE, 6th Ban, Oxford & Bucks (Pioneers) 7th Ban. Yorkshire Regt, and 5th Ban Duke of Cornwall's Light Infantry Q.E. I am granted leave from 29th to 5th inclusive. Capn Hughes my chief Clerk is taking charge near the supervision of the D.A.Q.M.G. He is quite capable of the work.	24 a3/

A. Fulcher Capt
ADVS 18th Division

18th Giri:
D.A.D.D.
Vol. 4

121/7635

25

Nov 15

Army Form C. 2118

WAR DIARY
or
INTELLIGENCE SUMMARY

(Erase heading not required.)

Confidential

WAR DIARY

OF

D.A.D.O.S. 18th DIVISION

From 1st November 1915 to 30th November 1915.

26

WAR DIARY or INTELLIGENCE SUMMARY

Army Form C. 2118

27

Place	Date	Hour	Summary of Events and Information	Remarks and references to Appendices
MELUL	6/11/15		Returned from leave	A.2
"	7/11/15		I found everything very satisfactory. Winter clothing coming along well with the exception of woollen vests - supplies of Nose bags has slightly improved but I have left chits out - there are improved nose bags but the muddy state of the front trenches has very soon caused them to break again.	
"	8/11/15		All units of the 26th & 27th Divisions have left. Some only partly completed their training - Sent to 12th Corps. Railhead for various stores left by them and which can be utilized.	
"	9/11/15			
"	10/11/15		Visit from DADGS 3rd Army.	

Army Form C. 2118

WAR DIARY
or
INTELLIGENCE SUMMARY
(Erase heading not required.)

28

Place	Date	Hour	Summary of Events and Information	Remarks and references to Appendices
HEILLY	11/5/15		The Thigh from Boots recently issued are proving a boon to the men in the trenches, the proportion allowed could with advantage be increased.	
-"-	12/5/15			
-"-	13/5/15			
-"-	14/5/15			
-"-	15/5/15			
-"-	16/5/15		M.Gen Ruthven - The following units have been placed under his command 96th and 99th French Attached for administrative purposes - No 6 Siege Coy Battalion, 152nd A.T. Company R.E. 170th ? and 179th Tunnelling Companies R.E.	

Army Form C. 2118

WAR DIARY
or
INTELLIGENCE SUMMARY

(Erase heading not required.)

Instructions regarding War Diaries and Intelligence Summaries are contained in F.S. Regs., Part II. and the Staff Manual respectively. Title Pages will be prepared in manuscript.

29

Place	Date	Hour	Summary of Events and Information	Remarks and references to Appendices
HEILLY	17/7			
"	18/7			
"	19/7			
"	20/7			
"	21/7			
"	22/7			
"	23/7			
"	24/7			
"	25/7			
"	26/7			

1875 Wt. W593/826 1,000,000 4/15 J.B.C. & A. A.D.S.S./Forms/C. 2118.

Army Form C. 2118

WAR DIARY
or
INTELLIGENCE SUMMARY
(Erase heading not required.)

Remarks and references to Appendices

30

Place	Date	Hour	Summary of Events and Information	Remarks and references to Appendices
HEILLY	27/4			
—	28/4			
—	29/4	10.5 a.m.	Travel Mortar Battery joined the Division	
—	30/4		Shoes coming about very satisfactory. Train Service bad. a.q. does not arrive till 9.30 p.m. which will mean d entraining	
	1/5		morning Service -	

A. Duleker Capt
bar'on 18th Div.

S.A.P. 18th brī:
rot: 5/6.
Dre

31

Confidential

War Diary

of

A.D.O.S. 18th Division

from 1st Dec 1915 to 31st December 1915

32

Place	Date	Hour	Summary of Events and Information	Remarks and references to Appendices
HEILLY	1/7		32nd Division Trains were joining this Division for training for Heavy Artillery - An effort made to communicate with Ordnance Supplies -	
"	2/7		Train 9/67 having late, I hear, the line I reorganized owing to a Railway accident at HANGEST -	Q.3
"	3/7		D.A.D.O.S. 32nd Division came over regarding issues to units of his Divn. - He decided to supply them in from his H.Q. Dump -	Q.3
"	4/7		Tempy. Lt. Vernall A.O.D. posted for an Ordnance tour of duty -	Q.3
"	5/7			Q.3
"	6/7		Tempy. Lt. Vernall A.O.D. proceeded for duty -	Q.3

33.

Army Form C. 2118

WAR DIARY
or
INTELLIGENCE SUMMARY
(Erase heading not required.)

Place	Date	Hour	Summary of Events and Information	Remarks and references to Appendices
HEILLY	7/7/15		W Battery RHA and 1 Section Ammunition Column joined this Division from 1st Indian Cavalry Division	a.9.
"	8/7/15		Orders received for GOC Smart to hold himself in readiness for a move.	a.9.
"	9/7/15			a.9.
"	10/7/15			a.9.
"	11/7/15		53rd Brigade are being relieved in the Trenches by 96th Inf Bde & are into rest at DAOURS and neighbourhood. 2nd Suffolk Regt relieved today – no alteration in output of Ordnance Stores to River banks until move is completed.	a.9.
"	12/7/15			a.9.

34

Army Form C. 2118

WAR DIARY
or
INTELLIGENCE SUMMARY

(Erase heading not required.)

Instructions regarding War Diaries and Intelligence Summaries are contained in F.S. Regs., Part II. and the Staff Manual respectively. Title Pages will be prepared in manuscript.

Place	Date	Hour	Summary of Events and Information	Remarks and references to Appendices
HEILLY	13/12/15			Q.9.
—„—	14/12/15		No 6 Ammunition Coln left for MARSIELLES.	
—„—	15/12/15		Orders received for D.A.D.O.S. Capt A. Fulcher to join at 1st Army Head Quarters on the 18th instant. Read VERNAU A.O.D. to take over duties of D.A.D.O.S.	—
—„—	16/12/15			Q.9.
—„—	17/12/15			Q.9.
—„—	18/12/15		Capt A Fulcher left for 1st Army Head Quarters. Lt Stephenson took over duties of D.A.D.O.S.	
—„—	19/12/15		Notified to forward all outstanding Indents for No 6 Ammunition Coln to Ordnance Officer Dieppe.	
—„—	20/12/15			Q.W
—„—	21/12/15			S.M

35

WAR DIARY
or
INTELLIGENCE SUMMARY

Army Form C. 2118

36

Place	Date	Hour	Summary of Events and Information	Remarks and references to Appendices
Hedey	22/12/15		Notified 99th French Tr. B.G. will be transferred to 32nd Div. on Jan 2nd – 16	
	23/12/15		53rd Infantry Brigade to replace 96th Inf. Bde. These will be carried out within the next few days.	
	24/12/15		[struck through line]	
	25/12/15		Insert No 5/3/19 containing Div. Stores in column at Salouel. See stores in Order	
			Correct.	
			No 2. Section D.A.C. moves to B. was under Orders O.C. D.A.C.	
	26/12/15		"	[initials]
	27/12/15		"	[initials]
	28/12/15		A.D.O.S. instead store. Details under other Instrns	
			H.Q. in 53rd Infantry Brigade, again at Albert	
	29/12/15		"	[initials]
	30/12/15		"	
	31/12/15		99th French Mortar Battery not to be transferred to 32 Div, by 32nd Div Orders	

37

WAR DIARY
or
INTELLIGENCE SUMMARY

Vol VI

Confidential
War Diary
of
A.D.O.S. 18th Division
from 1st Jan 1916 to 31st January 1916
Vol VI

Army Form C. 2118

WAR DIARY
or
INTELLIGENCE SUMMARY
(Erase heading not required.)

Instructions regarding War Diaries and Intelligence Summaries are contained in F. S. Regs., Part II. and the Staff Manual respectively. Title Pages will be prepared in manuscript.

Place	Date	Hour	Summary of Events and Information	Remarks and references to Appendices
Nilsey	1/1/6			
	2/1/6			
	3/1/6			
	4/1/6			
	5/1/6		253 Inspecting 67 R.E. Camp 18th Div. & Goum. 1st Army	
	6/1/6		Inspect Delousing Station & 7th H.Coy & Infantry Baths by any Enquiries of Officers who are investigating as to a new Anti-gas method and it seemed would offer their offers & so not claim a by his ?? accurate & time and other conditions.	
	7/1/6			
	8/1/6		Desc. Routine Orders Inspection & Delousing of Latrines & chemical testers by Lormer.	
	9/1/6			
	10/1/6			

38

WAR DIARY
or
INTELLIGENCE SUMMARY

Army Form C. 2118

(Erase heading not required.)

Instructions regarding War Diaries and Intelligence Summaries are contained in F. S. Regs., Part II. and the Staff Manual respectively. Title Pages will be prepared in manuscript.

Place	Date	Hour	Summary of Events and Information	Remarks and references to Appendices
Netley	11/1/16		Trailer D.D.O.S. 3rd Army. Regarding tft of Ack gun sergts and Ref to his O/99 d/29.11.15.	
	12/1/16		Everything satisfactory, working smoothly.	
	13/1/16		"	8am
	14/1/16			8am
	15/1/16			8.10
	16/1/16			8.00
	17/1/16			8.00
	18/1/16			8.10
	19/1/16			8.10
	20/1/16			8.10
	21/1/16		A.D.O.S. 10th Corps opr causes r officers m'cycle store	8.10
	22/1/16		D.D.O.S. 3rd Army m'cles store Bgs	8.10
	23/1/16			8.10
	24/1/16			
	25/1/16		Ordnance Conference A.D.O.S. 10th Corps 8am	
	26/1/16			

39

Place	Date	Hour	Summary of Events and Information	Remarks and references to Appendices
Heises	27/10			
	28/10		9AM D.A.D.O.S. of the Div. called on one informs me he is taking over my store for the Div. Have received no official notification of my Div. moving.	
	29/10		Arranged with D.A.D.O.S. 7th Div. to hand over of my store. 9PM	
	30/10		"	
	31/10		1 Warrant Officer & 6 men have arrived at my store for duty with 7th Div.	

DA/GS. 40A
18th Division
Vol VII

18 Div

Army Form C. 2118

WAR DIARY
or
INTELLIGENCE SUMMARY
(Erase heading not required.)

War Diary
of
D.A.D.O.S. 18th Div
for month of February 1916.

Army Form C. 2118

WAR DIARY
or
INTELLIGENCE SUMMARY
(Erase heading not required.)

Instructions regarding War Diaries and Intelligence Summaries are contained in F. S. Regs., Part II. and the Staff Manual respectively. Title Pages will be prepared in manuscript.

42

Place	Date	Hour	Summary of Events and Information	Remarks and references to Appendices
Heuzey	1/7/16		It has been heard that 18th Division are move to Kilkenant.	
	2/7/16		"	
	3/7/16		To Battery of 3rd Section Divisional Am Col. Colonne sur Ancre 18th Division Dinnants Scott, 2nd Lt Wilson to Div.	
			Informed 18th Div: a 6 men to Ribemont at 6 P.M. Left hospital & two wounded at G.E. rendezvous & not over noticed [wanting] of tom.	
	4/7/16		Arranged with Court Commandant at Ribemont & enable home evacuated men stores for the repair of the Armouries shops & occupying accommodation from Armouries shop to tomorrow. Courage & Lce Army Off. in Heuzey 8.30 am following morning.	
	5/7/16		Left Heuzey with O.C. H.Q. & few of number 9 A.M. all stores & our/part to move D.D.O.S. 2 Army, attend belated Stills Officers stores.	
Ribemont	6/7/16		Everything working very satisfactory; considering circumstances.	
	7/7/16		Move 142 Army Troops Coy RE from 18th Division to 9th Division	
	8/7/16		Move D/Battery 85th Brigade RFA from 18th Division to 55th Division West Lawn Trench 6y RE 20m 18th Division temporarily.	
	9/7/16		"	JM.
	10/7/16		A.D.O.S. 10th Corps called	
	11/7/16		Stores coming along very satisfactory, except Hourbags	

Army Form C. 2118

WAR DIARY
or
INTELLIGENCE SUMMARY
(Erase heading not required.)

43

Place	Date	Hour	Summary of Events and Information	Remarks and references to Appendices
Ribemont	12/7/16		Move 99th & 84th Trench Mortar Batteries from 18th Division to 55th Division by 18th Div. Train. 59th Field Coy RE 5th Div to be dismantled in journey by 19th Div. to Stores. 53rd, 55th Infantry Brigades Trench Mortar Gun batteries joins 18th Division.	
	13/7/16		Move 80th Field Coy RE from 18th Div. to 6 V.L Corps troops attd to them for operations. Three 3" Kite Balloon Sections from 18th Div to 4th Division	
	14/7/16		8 A.C.	
	15/7/16		8 A.D.	
	16/7/16		8 A.B.	
	17/7/16		proceeded in train to England	
	18/7/16		" "	8 A.A.
	19/7/16		" "	8 A.E.
	20/7/16		" "	8 A.J.
	21/7/16		" "	8 A.N.
	22/7/16		" "	8 A.M.
	23/7/16		84th Trench Mortar Battery joins 18th Division. Three 2nd West Lancs Field Coy RE rejoin 18th Div. 6 55th Division. Three 59th Field Coy RE from 18th Div. to 55th Division	8 V.D
	24/7/16		"	

Army Form C. 2118

WAR DIARY
or
INTELLIGENCE SUMMARY
(Erase heading not required.)

Place	Date	Hour	Summary of Events and Information	Remarks and references to Appendices
Rebemont	25/2/16		8pm	
	26/2/16		Returned from leave. Everything working satisfactorily 8pm	
	27/2/16		" 8pm	
	28/2/16		A.D.O.S. 10 AC on for council.	
	29/2/16		" 8pm	

44

WAR DIARY
or
INTELLIGENCE SUMMARY
(Erase heading not required.)

Army Form C. 2118

DADOS
18D
Vol 8

45

War Diary
of
D.A.D.O.S. 18th D
from 1st March to 31st March 16.

S. Herren Capt.
DADOS
18D
1/4/16

Army Form C. 2118

WAR DIARY
or
INTELLIGENCE SUMMARY
(Erase heading not required.)

Instructions regarding War Diaries and Intelligence Summaries are contained in F. S. Regs., Part II. and the Staff Manual respectively. Title Pages will be prepared in manuscript.

46

Place	Date	Hour	Summary of Events and Information	Remarks and references to Appendices
Rebremont	1 3/16		A.D.O.S. 13th Corps called	
	2 3/16		Move 92nd & 94th 105th French Mortar Btys & 15th to 7th & Bdy from 18th Div 6.32 Div.	
	3 3/16		Move C/85 Brigade R.T.A. from 18th Div to 30th Div.	
			" do	
	4 3/16		" do	
	5 3/16		99th French Mortar Bty. from 18th Div from 7th Div.	
Montigny	6 3/16		Div. H.Q. to move to Montigny. Arrangts for staff to be at Combres as there is no available place to be had in Montigny. 80th Lines 609 R.E. moves on 18th December	
	7 3/16		" do	
	8 3/16		Move 8th Rgy at Sweet Reserve from 18th Div to 4th Div. do	
	9 3/16		" do	
	10 3/16		" do	
	11 3/16		" do	
	12 3/16		" do	

Army Form C. 2118

WAR DIARY
or
INTELLIGENCE SUMMARY
(Erase heading not required.)

Instructions regarding War Diaries and Intelligence Summaries are contained in F.S. Regs., Part II and the Staff Manual respectively. Title Pages will be prepared in manuscript.

Place	Date	Hour	Summary of Events and Information	Remarks and references to Appendices
Montigny	13/3/16		92nd, 97th, & 105 Trench Mortar Batys. join 18th Div. from 32nd Div.	
	14/3/16		Syn	
	15/3/16		Syn	
	16/3/16		Move 442 Trench Mortar Battery from 3rd Army T Mortar School to 18th Div.	
	17/3/16		18th Division will move to Etinehem at the 20th inst: relieving there the 30th Div. area	
	18/3/16		Syn	
	19/3/16		Syn	
Etinehem	20/3/16		18th Div. move to Etinehem. Any stores in any way not suitable to convenient for moving etc.	
	21/3/16		Move 106 Entrenching Batt. & 135 Army Troops R.E. from 18th Div. to 6-7 & 30 Div.	
			Move 149 Tunnelling Coy R.E. from 18th Div. to 6 & 30 Div.	F 7
	22/3/16		Move 7th Entrenching Batt. & 119 Motor Machine Gun 8 Coy from 30th Div. to 18th Div.	
	23/3/16		Syn	
	24/3/16		Move 8 Irish Roman & 3rd Amb. Hoccer from 30th Div. to 18th Div.	
	25/3/16		Syn	
	26/3/16		Move 15 Motor Machine Gun Baty from 32nd Div. to 6/18 Div. and 18th Div. to 30th Div.	
	27/3/16		Do	

Army Form C. 2118

WAR DIARY
or
INTELLIGENCE SUMMARY

(Erase heading not required.)

Instructions regarding War Diaries and Intelligence Summaries are contained in F. S. Regs., Part II. and the Staff Manual respectively. Title Pages will be prepared in manuscript.

48

Place	Date	Hour	Summary of Events and Information	Remarks and references to Appendices
Etinehem	28/3/16		" Sys	
	29/3/16		" Sys	
	30/3/16		C 85th Brigade RFA sown 18th Division from 30th Division Syl	
	31/3/16		" Syl	

1875 Wt. W593/826 1,000,000 4/15 J.B.C. & A. A.D.S.S./Forms/C. 2118.

Army Form C. 2118

WAR DIARY
or
INTELLIGENCE SUMMARY
(Erase heading not required.)

Instructions regarding War Diaries and Intelligence Summaries are contained in F.S. Regs., Part II. and the Staff Manual respectively. Title Pages will be prepared in manuscript.

DADOS 18
Vol 9

49

Place	Date	Hour	Summary of Events and Information	Remarks and references to Appendices
Etinhem	1/4/16		" 9 M	
	2/4/16		" 9 M	
	3/4/16		Everything working smoothly	
	4/4/16		" 9 M	
	5/4/16		" 9 M	
	6/4/16		Move 1/4th Wheeling Coy R.E. from 30th Division to 18th Division	
	7/4/16		" 9 M	
	8/4/16		" 9 M	
	9/4/16		Stores are coming up well.	
	10/4/16		1/5th Kent Batty and 1/4th Home Counties Ammunition Columns join 18th Div.	
	11/4/16		Officer for the board of Survey have been detailed at this concentration as arranged at my Office for disposal of unfitting & condemning tents & clothing withdrawn from the troops. This A.R.O. sigds at 11.4.16.	
	13/4/16		" 9 M	
	14/4/16		" 9 M	
	15/4/16		" 9 M	
	16/4/16		Officers of the Board of Survey assembled at my Office 10 a.m. 53/2 and 55/2 French Mortar Batteries join 18th Division.	

Army Form C. 2118

WAR DIARY
or
INTELLIGENCE SUMMARY
(Erase heading not required.)

Instructions regarding War Diaries and Intelligence Summaries are contained in F. S. Regs., Part II. and the Staff Manual respectively. Title Pages will be prepared in manuscript.

Place	Date	Hour	Summary of Events and Information	Remarks and references to Appendices
Etricham	16/4/16		D.D.O.S. v^t Army and A.D.O.S. 13 Corps called & inspected mounted forward stores.	
	17/4/16		" " " "	
	18/4/16		" " " "	
	19/4/16		Move 1/4th Home Counties Amm Column and 1/5th Kent Batting How 4.5 from 18th Div. to 39th Division	
	20/4/16		36 Lewis Guns received. This number now complete for Infantry Battalions & S Guns.	
	21/4/16		" " " " "	
	22/4/16		" " " " "	
	23/4/16		" " " " "	
	24/4/16		" " " " "	
	25/4/16		" " " " "	
	26/4/16		Board of Survey assembled at my Office 10 a.m. to proceed to Enghien to inspect Horse Rugs.	8
	27/4/16		H.Q^{rs} of the Division is moving to Caureau on the 5th May. My Rations will be Longpré Railhead & trains.	
	28/4/16		Wires to D.A.D.O.S. 36th Division asking him in what we are taking over. I have arranged to take over his stores on the 5th May & also our Reservists.	

1875   Wt. W593/826   1,000,000   4/15   J.B.C. & A.   A.D.S.S./Forms/C. 2118.

Army Form C. 2118

WAR DIARY
or
INTELLIGENCE SUMMARY
(Erase heading not required.)

Place	Date	Hour	Summary of Events and Information	Remarks and references to Appendices
Etinehem	29/4/16		Move x1 Anti Aircraft Section from 9th Division to 18th Division	51
	30/4/16		Owing to the considerable advance Railhead was to form my Dump on the 3rd, 4th, & 5th May 16, it will be impossible for me to collect stores. I have therefore written home asking them to suspend all issues of stores which were to arriving at Railhead on the 1st ayo.	

Army Form C. 2118

DADOS
18th
Vol 10

52

WAR DIARY
or
INTELLIGENCE SUMMARY
(Erase heading not required.)

War Diary
of
D.A.D.O.S. 18th Division
for
Month of May 1915.

WAR DIARY or INTELLIGENCE SUMMARY

Army Form C. 2118

Place	Date	Hour	Summary of Events and Information	Remarks and references to Appendices
Erimhem	1/5/16		"	
	2/5/16		"	
	3/5/16		"	
	4/5/16		Move of Entrenching Battalion, 14th Tunnelling Coy RE and 3rd Ambulance Flotilla from 18th Division to 30th Division. Move of 6 Hordenks Regt from 18th Division to 4th Army Troops.	
Acey Sur Somme	5/5/16		Moved Officers & Men & Horses from Entrenchm Bn from - Acey-sur-Somme, from 6 Hordenks from 4th Army Troops to 18th Division.	
	6/5/16		" do	
	7/5/16		" do	
	8/5/16		" do	
	9/5/16		"	
	10/5/16		Move XL Anti-Aircraft Section from 18th Div to 30th Division. A.D.O.S. called inspected stores. V 18 Heavy Trench Mortar Battery joins 18th Division	
	11/5/16			
	12/5/16		Move 15th Motor Machine Gun Battery from 18th Division to 15th Corps troops. Move 18th Divisional Cavalry Squadron from 18th Division to 4th Army Troops.	53
	13/5/16		A.D.O.S. 13th Corps called. do	

Army Form C. 2118

WAR DIARY
or
INTELLIGENCE SUMMARY
(Erase heading not required.)

Instructions regarding War Diaries and Intelligence Summaries are contained in F.S. Regs, Part II. and the Staff Manual respectively. Title Pages will be prepared in manuscript.

54

Place	Date	Hour	Summary of Events and Information	Remarks and references to Appendices
Silly sur Somme	14/5/16		Supplies coming up well	
	15/5/16	8 AM	"	
	16/5/16	8 AM	"	
	17/5/16	8 AM	"	
	18/5/16		Leave of Absence has been approved for me from the 19th June. Lt Parker A.O.D. was holding O.A.D.O.S.	
			Move A B and C Squadrons H/ Northumberland Hussars from 7th Division, 1st Division and 6th Divisions respectively, to 18th Division.	
	19/5/16	8 AM	"	
	20/5/16	8 AM	"	
	21/5/16	9 AM	"	
	22/5/16		Move 18th Divisional Cyclist Coy from 18th Division to 13th Corps Troops.	
	23/5/16	8 AM	"	
	24/5/16	8 AM	"	
	25/5/16		Move W.18 Heavy Trench Mortar Battery from 19th Division	
	26/5/16	8 AM		

1875 Wt. W593/826 1,000,000 4/15 J.B.C. & A. A.D.S.S./Forms/C. 2118.

Army Form C. 2118

WAR DIARY
or
INTELLIGENCE SUMMARY

(Erase heading not required.)

Instructions regarding War Diaries and Intelligence Summaries are contained in F. S. Regs., Part II. and the Staff Manual respectively. Title Pages will be prepared in manuscript.

55

Place	Date	Hour	Summary of Events and Information	Remarks and references to Appendices
Arry Sur Somme	27/5/16		8pm	
	28/5/16	"	Returned from leave. 8pm	
	29/5/16	"	8pm	
	30/5/16	"	8pm	
	31/5/16	"	8pm	

Army Form C. 2118

WAR DIARY
or
INTELLIGENCE SUMMARY

(Erase heading not required.)

Instructions regarding War Diaries and Intelligence Summaries are contained in F. S. Regs., Part II. and the Staff Manual respectively. Title Pages will be prepared in manuscript.

DADOS 18 Div

Place	Date	Hour	Summary of Events and Information	Remarks and references to Appendices
				56
				VGG 12 June

War Diary
for
the Month of June 16

J W Annas Lt Col
DADOS
18 Div

1/7/16

1875 Wt. W593/826 1,000,000 4/15 J.B.C. & A. A.D.S.S./Forms/C. 2118.

Army Form C. 2118

WAR DIARY
or
INTELLIGENCE SUMMARY
(Erase heading not required.)

Instructions regarding War Diaries and Intelligence Summaries are contained in F.S. Regs., Part II. and the Staff Manual respectively. Title Pages will be prepared in manuscript.

57

Place	Date	Hour	Summary of Events and Information	Remarks and references to Appendices
Army in Somme	1/6/16		Bn	
	2/6/16		Bn	
	3/6/16		Conference at A.D.O.S. 13th Corps Office	
	4/6/16	"	"	
	5/6/16	"	Bn	
	6/6/16	"	Bn	
	7/6/16	"	Bn	
	8/6/16	"	Bn	
	9/6/16	"	Bn	
	10/6/16	"	Bn	
	11/6/16	"	Bn	
	12/6/16	"	Bn	
	13/6/16	"	Bn	
	14/6/16	"	Bn	
	15/6/16	"	Bn	
	16/6/16	"	Bn	
	17/6/16			

W/18 Warrant Mordan Battery Joins 18th Div Officers & Stores now at Corbie.

Army Form C. 2118

WAR DIARY
or
INTELLIGENCE SUMMARY
(Erase heading not required.)

Instructions regarding War Diaries and Intelligence Summaries are contained in F. S. Regs., Part II. and the Staff Manual respectively. Title Pages will be prepared in manuscript.

58

Place	Date	Hour	Summary of Events and Information	Remarks and references to Appendices
Basra	18/6/16		Sd.	
	19/6/16		Sd.	
	20/6/16		Sd.	
	21/6/16		Move 1/1 Northumberland Hussars to 13 Corps troops from 18th Div	
	22/6/16		Sd.	
	23/6/16		Sd.	
	24/6/16		Sd.	
	25/6/16		Sd.	
	26/6/16		Transfer Motor Machine Gun Batty from 18th Div to 13 Corps troops	
	27/6/16		"	
	28/6/16		"	
	29/6/16		"	
	30/6/16		"	

18/ Vol 12

59

D.A.D.O.S.
18TH DIVISION.

Army Form C. 2118

WAR DIARY
or
INTELLIGENCE SUMMARY
(Erase heading not required.)

War Diary of
D.A.D.O.S.
18th Div:

For the month of Aug. 1916.

J. Hamer
for
D.A.D.O.S
18 Div
6/16

60

HEADQUARTERS
6 AUG 1916
18th DIVISION

Army Form C. 2118

WAR DIARY
or
INTELLIGENCE SUMMARY
(Erase heading not required.)

Instructions regarding War Diaries and Intelligence Summaries are contained in F. S. Regs., Part II. and the Staff Manual respectively. Title Pages will be prepared in manuscript.

61

Place	Date	Hour	Summary of Events and Information	Remarks and references to Appendices
Barce	1/1/16		" 2 M.	
	2/1/16		" 8 M.	
	3/1/16		" 2 M.	
	4/1/16		Stores coming up well, with the exception of Spring Running Out 1865, and Steel Heads. Iron not to letter as not available at present. 8 M.	
	5/1/16		" 8 M.	
	6/1/16		I called on I.O.M. Heavy Trestle Workshop for 3 2" Hand Mortars and spare parts.	
	7/1/16		" 8 M.	
	8/1/16		" 8 M.	
	9/1/16		Called in Heavy Trestle Workshop for 1st Inspection Base Workshop for 2" Mortars	
	10/1/16		A.D.O.S. 13 about to called at my Office 8 M.	
	11/1/16		" 8 M.	
	12/1/16		" 8 M.	
	13/1/16		Spring Running Out O-ring coming up much better.	
	14/1/16		" 8 M.	
	15/1/16		" 8 M.	
	16/1/16			
	17/1/16		1/18 Trench Mortar Battery disbanded. Arranged over hand to return stores and equipment as early as possible.	

WAR DIARY
or
INTELLIGENCE SUMMARY

Army Form C. 2118

(Erase heading not required.)

Place	Date	Hour	Summary of Events and Information	Remarks and references to Appendices
Corbie	18/7/16		"	
	19/7/16		8pm	
	20/7/16		8pm	
	21/7/16		Divisional HQ move to Haircourt. Sent off my 3 Bde W.O. who then went to Sorel	
	22/7/16		Office Staff and HQ Group move to Haircourt	
	23/7/16		Division leaves 13 Corps and goes 5 Corps. Move to Rainneau	
Haircourt	23/7/16			
Rainneau	24/7/16		" 8pm	
	25/7/16		" 8pm	
	26/7/16		Based on A.D.O.S. 5th Corps and J.O.M. 5th Corps	
	27/7/16		Based on Div Artillery HQrs, 82nd and 83rd Bde HQrs, R. Lewis's for Ammo etc	
	28/7/16		1 m/s HQ Full — 65th Bde R.F.A.	
	29/7/16		Division is now temporarily attached to II Anzac Corps - A.D.O.S.	
	30/7/16		II Anzac Corps called) 8pm	
	31/7/16		" 8pm	

62

63

War Diary of D.A.D.O.S. 18 Div.
for the hours of August 16

O Harrett Capt
for D.A.D.O.S.
18 Div
3/9/16

Army Form C. 2118

WAR DIARY
or
INTELLIGENCE SUMMARY
(Erase heading not required.)

Instructions regarding War Diaries and Intelligence Summaries are contained in F. S. Regs., Part II. and the Staff Manual respectively. Title Pages will be prepared in manuscript.

Place	Date	Hour	Summary of Events and Information	Remarks and references to Appendices

Army Form C. 2118

WAR DIARY
or
INTELLIGENCE SUMMARY
(Erase heading not required.)

Instructions regarding War Diaries and Intelligence Summaries are contained in F. S. Regs., Part II. and the Staff Manual respectively. Title Pages will be prepared in manuscript.

64

Place	Date	Hour	Summary of Events and Information	Remarks and references to Appendices
Reninure	1/8/16		8th	
	2/8/16		Div move to (Rang-dur-Bac. Moved close to factory	
Bouzin court 3/8/16			situated near Bac St Maur. 8th	
	4/8/16		" 8th	
	5/8/16		A.D.O.S. 2nd Anzac Corps called.	
	6/8/16		Survey Reached Bac St Maur	
	7/8/16		" 8th	
	8/8/16		" 8th	
	9/8/16		" 8th	
	10/8/16		" 8th	
	11/8/16		Pte D---- 6th Royal Berkshire Regt. wounded in not on foot was killed by shell fire 1:45 pm Goog. Also 2 men was slightly wounded, but after dressing landing they went able to carry out their duties	
	12/8/16		" 8th	
	13/8/16		" 8th	
	14/8/16		" 6th	
	15/8/16		" 8th	

Army Form C. 2118

WAR DIARY
or
INTELLIGENCE SUMMARY
(Erase heading not required.)

Instructions regarding War Diaries and Intelligence Summaries are contained in F. S. Regs., Part II. and the Staff Manual respectively. Title Pages will be prepared in manuscript.

65

Place	Date	Hour	Summary of Events and Information	Remarks and references to Appendices
Corps du Bac	16/8/16		" " 8tt	
	17/8/16		D.D.O.S. 2nd Army and A.D.O.S. 2nd Anzac Corps called at my Office	
	18/8/16		Visited 2nd Army Hortatops.	
	19/8/16		Owing to reduction now of the formation to 3rd Army arrangements were made to greatest value of stores from saloon of our 21st not needed further action from me.	
	20/8/16		" " 8tt	
	21/8/16		Visit by A.D.O.S. 2nd Anzac Corps	
	22/8/16		" " 8n	
	23/8/16		" " 8tt	
Bavincourt	24/8/16		Divisional HQrs move to Bavincourt	
Rocquencourt	25/8/16		Divisional HQrs move to Rocquencourt, 3rd Army Area.	
	26/8/16		" " 8tt	
	27/8/16		Visit by A.D.O.S. 19th Corps	
	28/8/16		Visit by D.D.O.S. 3rd Army.	
	29/8/16		" " 8tt	
	30/8/16		" "	
	31/8/16		The unit of the Divisional Artillery and HQrs of 18 Div Home have been transferred attached to 15 August Corps. 8tt	

WAR DIARY
or
INTELLIGENCE SUMMARY

Army Form C. 2118

VOL 14

HEAD QUARTERS
No. 9 OCT 1916
18TH DIVISION

66

ADMS 18 Div.

Place	Date	Hour	Summary of Events and Information	Remarks and references to Appendices
Rossignol	1/9/16		8th Royal Sussex Pioneers transferred to 49th Division from 18th Division	
	2/9/16		" " Inf	
	3/9/16		" " Bde	
	4/9/16		" " Bde	
	5/9/16		" " Bde	
	6/9/16		" " Ind	
	7/9/16		" " Ind	
	8/9/16		" " Bn	
Domestoro	9/9/16		Divisional HQ move to Domestoro	
	10/9/16		Tools A.D.O.S. z "6oofs"	
Achiens	11/9/16		Divisional HQ moves to Achiens. The 18th Div. Artillery transferred to the Division from 1st Canadian Div.	
	12/9/16		Tools HQ Divisional Artillery	
	13/9/16		" " Inf	
	14/9/16		HQ on by 18th Div Division transferred to 158th Div from 1st Canadian Inf. Brigade	
	15/9/16		" " Bn	
	16/9/16		" " Bde	
	17/9/16		" " Ind	
	18/9/16		Local on A.D.O.S. z "6oofs"	
	19/9/16		" Bn	

WAR DIARY or INTELLIGENCE SUMMARY

Army Form C. 2118

(Erase heading not required.)

Instructions regarding War Diaries and Intelligence Summaries are contained in F. S. Regs., Part II. and the Staff Manual respectively. Title Pages will be prepared in manuscript.

Place	Date	Hour	Summary of Events and Information	Remarks and references to Appendices
Acheux	20/9/16		Ord.	
	21/9/16		Ord.	
	22/9/16		Ord.	
	23/9/16		Ord.	
	24/9/16		Ord.	
			49th Div Artillery HQrs, 146 Infantry Brigade, 5th W Yorks Regt, 6th W Yorks, 7 W Yorks, 8 W Yorks, 146 Trench Mortar Bty. 1/1 W R Field Ambulance, 1/2 W R Field Bty R.E. No 1 & 2 Coy 49 Div Train and 49th Mobile Veteran transferred to this Division. 2000 Steyn Gum Boots received.	
	25/9/16		8th Royal Sussex Pioneers, 119th Field Coy R.E., 244 Field Coy R.E., 7/49, 249 + 449, 549 and 5/49 Trench Mortar Batteries transferred to this Div from 49th Div. Div numerar HQrs moved to Hedauville. A.D.O.S z infantry cadres.	
	26/9/16		Ord.	
	27/9/16		Ord.	
	28/9/16		Ord.	
	29/9/16		146 Inf Bde, O.C., 6th, 7, 4 and 8 W Yorks, 146 Trench Mortar Bty, 1/1 W R Field Ambulance, 1/2 W R Field Coy R.E. and 49 Div Train transferred to 49 Division.	
	30/9/16		Ord.	

67

Army Form C. 2118

Vol # 15

WAR DIARY
or
INTELLIGENCE SUMMARY
(Erase heading not required.)

68

HEAD QUARTERS
5 NOV 1916
63rd DIVISION

Place	Date	Hour	Summary of Events and Information	Remarks and references to Appendices
Hedauville	1/10/16		bts	
	2/10/16		" bts	
	3/10/16		Move 49th Divn. 310th R.A. 310th Ammunition Column, No 1, 2, 3 and 4 Sections D.A.C. HQrs & HQ Coy Divnl, 49th Mobile Vet Section, 245, 246, 247 Brigades HQrs and A, B, C & D Batteries and 248 Brigade HQrs and A, B & C Batteries from 18th Division to 49th Division. Move 1/5 West Yorkshire Regt, U, W, X, Y and Z Trench Mortar Batteries from 18th Division to 49th Division. 8000 Yeugh Gum Boots transferred to 39th Division.	
	4/10/16		bts	
	5/10/16		"	
	6/10/16		Divn. HQrs move to Bertrancourt	
Bertrancourt	7/10/16		Move No 3 Ammn. Sub Park from 18th Divn. to 5th Corps Troops. bts	
	8/10/16		" bts	
	9/10/16		" bts	
	10/10/16		Move X & Y/18 Trench Mortar Btys from 18th Divn. to 51st Division. Special cash granted to men.	
	11/10/16		" bts	

1875 Wt. W593/826 1,000,000 4/15 J.B.C. & A. A.D.S.S./Forms/C. 2118.

Army Form C. 2118

WAR DIARY
or
INTELLIGENCE SUMMARY

(Erase heading not required.)

Volume XIII

Instructions regarding War Diaries and Intelligence Summaries are contained in F.S. Regs., Part II. and the Staff Manual respectively. Title Pages will be prepared in manuscript.

HEAD QUARTERS
5 NOV 1916
18th DIVISION

69

Place	Date	Hour	Summary of Events and Information	Remarks and references to Appendices
Daours	12/10/16		Move 119 Railway Coy R.E. from 18th Div. to 2 Corps troops.	
	13/10/16		"	
	14/10/16		"	
	15/10/16		"	
	16/10/16		"	
	17/10/16		Div. H.Quarters to Albert	
Albert	18/10/16		"	
	19/10/16		"	
	20/10/16		"	
	21/10/16		Returns from Units	
	22/10/16		"	
	23/10/16		"	
	24/10/16		"	
	25/10/16		"	
	26/10/16		"	
	27/10/16		"	
	28/10/16		"	
	29/10/16		"	
	30/10/16		Move 32nd Machine Gun Coy from 11th Div. to 18th Division	
	31/10/16		"	

J. Morgan Lieut. Col.
D.A.D.O.S. 18th DIVISION

1875 Wt. W593/826 1,000,000 4/15 J.B.C. & A. A.D.S.S./Forms/C. 2118.

WAR DIARY or INTELLIGENCE SUMMARY

Army Form C. 2118

19/1995
18th/Ans.
Volume XIV

Jul/16

Place	Date	Hour	Summary of Events and Information	Remarks and references to Appendices
Front	1/7/16		Taken on A.D.O.S. 2nd Corps.	70
	2/7/16		"	
	3/7/16		"	
	4/7/16		"	
	5/7/16		Stores coming up well	
	6/7/16		"	
	7/7/16		"	
	8/7/16		"	
	9/7/16		"	
	10/7/16		"	
	11/7/16		"	
	12/7/16		"	
	13/7/16		"	
	14/7/16		No. 1 & No. 14 Div. R.A. 78th Bde & Div. A.B.& D. Bdes. 19 Div on A.B.6 & D. Bdes. 81st Bde & No. A.D. R. Bdes. 19 Div on column Nos 1, 2, 3, 4 Balloon Bdes. Div. Heavy Trench Mortar Bdy. X, Y, Z Medium Trench Mortar Bdy. and No. 1 by 14 Div. C. Srown transferred to 18 Div from 39 Div.	
	15/7/16			
	16/7/16		32nd Machine Gun Cy transferred to 32nd Div from 18th Division	
	17/7/16		X + Y + Z Medium Trench Mortar Bdys transferred from 31st Div to 18 Div.	
	18/7/16			

Army Form C. 2118

WAR DIARY
or
INTELLIGENCE SUMMARY

(Erase heading not required.)

Instructions regarding War Diaries and Intelligence Summaries are contained in F. S. Regs., Part II. and the Staff Manual respectively. Title Pages will be prepared in manuscript.

71

Place	Date	Hour	Summary of Events and Information	Remarks and references to Appendices
Albert	19/11/16		"	
	20/11/16		"	
	21/11/16		HQrs 1st Div R.A. yth and 49th Bn ANDs & A.B.C & D Btys 34th Div 51st Bde R.F.A. and A B & D Btys HQrs 1st D.A.C. and Nos 1, 2, 3, & 4 Sections D.A.C. Try Heavy 9 m A By X, Y, Z Trys H.Q and J.Tr Btys and No 1 Coy 1st Div Train transferred to 1st Division from 1st Division.	
Bucquoy	22/11/16		Division began to move back to Rest Area, 7, 8, 9 Batteries. Division moved to Fonquoy. L. moved up with Note on the Refusing of the Division HQrs moved from the line, I move to Bucquoy and selected a forward Dump.	
to Foncquevillers	23/11/16		"	
	24/11/16		"	
	25/11/16		"	
	26/11/16		"	
	27/11/16		"	
	28/11/16		"	
	29/11/16		"	
	30/11/16		"	

Vol 17

72

Confidential

War Diary
of
A.D.O.S. 18th Div.

from 1 to 31 December 1916.

Army Form C. 2118.

WAR DIARY
or
INTELLIGENCE SUMMARY.
(Erase heading not required.)

Instructions regarding War Diaries and Intelligence Summaries are contained in F. S. Regs., Part II. and the Staff Manual respectively. Title pages will be prepared in manuscript.

73

Place	Date	Hour	Summary of Events and Information	Remarks and references to Appendices
Burying St Thadow	1. 12/16			
	2. 12/16		"	
	3. 12/16		"	
	4. 12/16		"	
	5. 12/16		Stores coming up well.	
	6. 12/16		"	
	7. 12/16		Called on I.O.M. No 28 Ordnance Workshop. Arrangements made with I.O.M.C. input all vehicles convoired by truckto to be overhauled.	
	8. 12/16		"	
	9. 12/16		Called on A.A.O.S. 2nd Corps.	
	10. 12/16		"	
	11. 12/16		I.O.M. inspected Vehicles, referred to above.	
	12. 12/16		"	
	13. 12/16		"	
	14. 12/16		"	
	15. 12/16		Called on 53rd 54th and 55th Bde MGC.	

Army Form C. 2118.

WAR DIARY
or
INTELLIGENCE SUMMARY.
(Erase heading not required.)

Instructions regarding War Diaries and Intelligence Summaries are contained in F. S. Regs., Part II. and the Staff Manual respectively. Title pages will be prepared in manuscript.

74

Place	Date	Hour	Summary of Events and Information	Remarks and references to Appendices
Bugny St Maclou	16/12/16			
	17/12/16		"	
	18/12/16		Visited I.O.M. No 28 Ordnance Workshop.	
	19/12/16		"	
	20/12/16		"	
	21/12/16		"	
	22/12/16		"	
	23/12/16		"	
	24/12/16		Visited A.D.O.S 2 Corps and Ordnance Workshop.	
	25/12/16		"	
	26/12/16			
	27/12/16		Director Ordnance has instructed me to report to Ordnance H.Qrs, 3rd Army at once, for temporary duty with Heavy Section Machine Gun Corps.	

75

DADOS/8/2
Vol 18

76

WAR DIARY
or
INTELLIGENCE SUMMARY
(Erase heading not required.)

Army Form C. 2118

Place	Date 1917	Hour	Summary of Events and Information	Remarks and references to Appendices
Bisigny N. Meadow	Jan 1		Visitors Richard - H. Kingson. Find that only very few H.J. Corks were L/Cpl H.J. in charge must no idea as to what to do with anything re. Visitors MAPS. L/Cpl discussed several things with him, including the question of sods now rifles having been returned to Infantry of any sort:-	
	2		Visit H.Q of the 3 Infantry Brigades, all of them satisfied. 15th Bple gave me but opinion in connection all others very too ill to settle merits of the three kinds methods. Inspector F.S. Bae thinks of shortage of Hosp in this method.	
	3		Several Routine. Store coming which will revolt longer hurts.	
	2		took of Div. Artillery & H.Q. Coy rel. Rain seems to be area & are starter to MAP to Div.	
	4		MAPS S. Div. called, as he is taking over my store when we move.	
	5		"	
	6		Inspection out of whole charger parts for Fred HAP. Ft. Garroday to fix we weekly return of undercloths, den & with. This should give some idea of composition of those stores.	
	7		Inspection Stores in view of move to forward area	

WAR DIARY or INTELLIGENCE SUMMARY

Army Form C. 2118.

Place	Date 1917	Hour	Summary of Events and Information	Remarks and references to Appendices
Busseboom / Shadow	Jan 8		Moved 28th Sanitary Section to 11 with Trench, as they are not going out with the Division.	77
"	9		Visited O.C. N.Z.S., who orders ceased with his Staff etc. the question of Trench to be brought up by him re & lot of kitted Q.D. & horse Shoes & takeover training Sections of Shoes to be left behind	
"	10		Moved 92. field Coy R.E. from 1/3 Division	
"	11		Division began during forward area	
"	12		Division marching	
"	13		Ditto Ditto	
"	14		Ditto Ditto	
"	15		Transferred 1st School 1 to 11 to Div.	
Helenville			Moved Offices Himself to Helenville. Subdivision to Divil only R.E. 1/5 RE.s (Pioneer Bn) Sanitary Section Staff 13 E. N° & 236 A.T. Coys R.E. were also distributed out & 136.E N° 102 field Coys R.E. (63 Div) & 94 labour Bn. R.E. — in lower two (Pioneers 1/3 Div) 18 Div & to M.G. Coy have been returned to me this command & evac. - Clicks have left for the	
"	16			

Army Form C. 2118.

WAR DIARY
or
INTELLIGENCE SUMMARY.
(Erase heading not required.)

78

Place	Date	Hour	Summary of Events and Information	Remarks and references to Appendices
Hebuterne	Mar 17		General Routine	
	18		Intra Brigade relief	
	19		Baths resumed. cleaning of trenches in with R.T.O. orders	
	20		200 stores arrived	
	21		Large quantity of stores arrived at Bde HQrs including 78 whls - staff having of bdl Div reported one new man - Brigade H.Q. staff having of bdl Div reported one new man - At the hrs Arty Co from reported one Div	
	22		General Routine	
	23		[illegible] 103 Field Coys & 16 (Lowestoft) Pioneers to 56 (RN) Div. Baths kept open continually turned out from Baths without Hanitis - four carrs without porters to fin tents - speed handed in such better area this. need to have urgently for 500 r honoured 300 from HQ Md meanwhile. traffic also went out without bow Ruhin for mothers having made an award	
	24		moves bn HQ HE to bn HQ	
	25		Discussed with Stoff pl of informal quarters of clean clothing from divisional laundry in Authille. Arranged to let up for no	

Army Form C. 2118.

WAR DIARY
or
INTELLIGENCE SUMMARY.

(Erase heading not required.)

Instructions regarding War Diaries and Intelligence Summaries are contained in F. S. Regs., Part II. and the Staff Manual respectively. Title pages will be prepared in manuscript.

79

Place	Date	Hour	Summary of Events and Information	Remarks and references to Appendices
Hedwa Dispersal	1916 26		Trouble with transport &c. To be further discussed later. Moved 2 36 M.T. Coy, M.E. to Didwana & Cairo Troops. Conference with ADMS.	
	27 28		Granted leave to homesick Englnd for 10 days. Details being carried on Expdt Throughout - till Coy Officers &c. will be present on leave now to completion on Trench railways	
	29 30		A.D.M.S. to Cairo visited stores convoys &c with Indries. Do Genl Ascond Infantry Bgde Spring's letter re Zurich (Byde) Eross Country	
	31		Two stores from Suez. Reconnaissance fund ADMS to Dri	

WAR DIARY
or
INTELLIGENCE SUMMARY

Army Form C. 2118.

18th Division

18th D. Train

D.A.D.O.S   Vol/9

(Erase heading not required.)

Place	Date	Hour	Summary of Events and Information	Remarks and references to Appendices
Neluville	1/2/17		Proceeded on leave.	
	14/2/17		Returned from leave. Found that much of the office had been moved. A.D.O.S. had visited office during my absence.	
	15			
	16/18		Removal of No. 1 Shifts Railway Section from house. General Routine work.	
	18			
	19		[illegible handwritten entry spanning multiple lines]	
	20/22			
	19 23			
	27 28			

Army Form C. 2118.

WAR DIARY
or
INTELLIGENCE SUMMARY.
(Erase heading not required.)

Davos
18th Div.

Vol 20

81

Place	Date	Hour	Summary of Events and Information	Remarks and references to Appendices
Bouzincourt	1917 Feb 1-14		Visited billets & dug-outs throughout. Various questions with [illegible]. [illegible] Probable for site of church near Senlecourt of D.HQ.	
			General Routine	
	9		Moved 9 Platoon Bn to 63 Div.	
	20		23 ORs sent 6s of Offrs wounded	
	21		318 Army 7 O. Bn to joined	
	22		Moved following to Military Cords	
			138 H.T. Coy R.E. 20 Platoon Bn 9th D. Riff	
			WS do. 1 Platoon Coy R.E. Div.	
			2 A. Ful Rly Transfer Coy 18 Coy I.W.W.R. Corps	
			309 Road Construction Coy	
			313 do.	
	20		Individual Orders.	
	22		Orders not being carried out by [illegible] to encourage	
	23		stores received relative to [illegible] forward [illegible] of officers.	
Meaulte	26 27		Moved to Meaulte - and [illegible]	
			X 18 D. [illegible] & 9 Div.	

Army Form C. 2118.

WAR DIARY
or
INTELLIGENCE SUMMARY.
(Erase heading not required.)

Instructions regarding War Diaries and Intelligence Summaries are contained in F. S. Regs., Part II. and the Staff Manual respectively. Title pages will be prepared in manuscript.

82

Place	Date	Hour	Summary of Events and Information	Remarks and references to Appendices
Merseyside	25/38		2 new stores arriving.	
	26		5 Reinforcement Inspection. New draft up to establishment.	
			Issued 64 & 315. Army J.B. Belts to 51 Bn	
			" 23 " " " 9 "	
	27		Stores arriving	Wherever [illegible] Lt Col. [illegible]

B.O.W.R.   Scott

Herewith War Diary
for April 1917

Lt Col ? ?
O C DoS

30/4/17

WAR DIARY
or
INTELLIGENCE SUMMARY.

(Erase heading not required.)

Army Form C. 2118.

April 1917

DA190A

18th Div.

Place	Date	Hour	Summary of Events and Information	Remarks and references to Appendices
Henencourt	1917			
	1		Gunners morning. Battery Commanders calling in to Store — munitions urgently required	
	2			
	3			
	4		2nd Lt H.H.H. at Hove returned from Rest. 2nd Lt P.J. Elfmore called in. 2nd Lt J.N. Jolly to Havre returned for 3 weeks. Sent him to Iw.S. fd. workshops — time for this relief.	
	5		Very damaged poor work to refit to Scale	
	18		Major Kinneer went to 48 Bn. They gather had Orders to move a colour head — Thus gathered that very hospitable from home tho I him he liked.	
			That 79 Bn S. A. J. J. D. to be refractive — to be [illegible] to be refractive —	
			Moved 79 Batt boy not huzzah to be up. They engaged to receive such clothing for Relief at Stratsage is next to them there other week. Return to	
	22		Moved to Dernauville. Received 16700 rounds of ammunition	
	29		Moved to Dernauville	

83

84

Secret

18 Div. D.

Herewith war diary for
[month]

3/4/17

A Woodson Lieut
O.S.O.S.

ack.
4/6 Jan

WAR DIARY
or
INTELLIGENCE SUMMARY.

Army Form C. 2118.

18th Division
May 1917

Place	Date	Hour	Summary of Events and Information	Remarks and references to Appendices
Rainneville	May 1		Arrived from Rubempré	
	2		Inspected P.T.V.T. VII Corps. Staff left 30 o'c RA.	
	5		Horse showing which ran very hrs.	
			Arrangements for machine guns re. personnel investigated inside Brigades	
Le Meillard	15		Move to HQ from chat Marpe	
Bouquemaison	22		Remove Store to Bouquemaison Mont	
	23		30 M.W. R.H. moved to do own Div	
	24		General routine	
	31			

Acknowledged
offrs to div

WAR DIARY or INTELLIGENCE SUMMARY

Army Form C. 2118.

DAP/S 18th Nov July 1917

Place	Date 1917	Hour	Summary of Events and Information	Remarks and references to Appendices
Corrin July	1		Instructions from Brit. after 2nd 7/5/17 - Every leaving this Hindney from Marine Base	86
Hawthorne	4		Moved to Hawthorne Moved to Rumphelf. High over the base absorbing a catastrophe 6 M and 30 bis. Moved distances	
Rum Halob	6		Force arrived from Cairo	
	7		Moved to Rumphelf Dis. - so I yield for 2 3. the few days else 30 the latter of very stringent life both in 10 days line consolidated power to must - F.E button encampment forme	
	9		Returned from leave	
	20		Moved 3 o'on P.N. + R.F. 6:30 P.M. 1 Aust. bitn to us	
	21			
	28/7 31/5		thus generally arrivers quickly from base & very satisfactory from Gun Park. Even otherwise for move is hostile as some in town were division have written had fewer stores sent out	

Whoursom Cobb. CRM T.S.B

WAR DIARY
or
INTELLIGENCE SUMMARY

Army Form C. 2118.

Vol 25
August 1917.

Place	Date	Hour	Summary of Events and Information	Remarks
Reninghelst huts	1917 5		Received Orders at Dickebusch – F.D. Clothing Socks being very urgently required – wrote Calais sent 7 lorries down – obtaining 1000 Suits S.D. 2000 prs Socks – also 1,000 prs Boots	
			Received hairdown	
	14 6		Stores coming up very quickly – Received 1 amb: pkt kit 5 – No 1. amb: km: sub Park – 20.9 Army Issues to R.E. – 2nd Canadian Divisional Supply Coy – to 10. Sp.d.	
	14		husband stone from 13000	
			Issued to Kemmel Shelter	
	15		Most invalids done – Completed move	
	17		Conferences of Office held – other items RE	
	18		manages to Reliever Stores by lorry to RF units & other BEF arranged with S.S. Both units at refilling point – Distributed dead Oil had to be refitted by lorry by 23/8. Informed Calais as to purpose for stores by rwy in case of rupture – Unwounded position at Continues. In Enduring fully capacity – Ammunition Storage for 9mm mags given in depot Box Respirators – 3 men Canteens & Spare Spindles	
	19 20		Best Truss Trestles – 3 men Canteens & Spare Spindles	
	19		Trestles Ju Bal all Bath stuck Lay se in factor of Rifles when machine guns re-ordered.	

87

Army Form C. 2118.

WAR DIARY
or
INTELLIGENCE SUMMARY.
(Erase heading not required.)

88

Place	Date	Hour	Summary of Events and Information	Remarks and references to Appendices
Fubergute	Aug 23		Conference of C.Os.	
	27		Visited 1/3 Bedf. M.G. Coys - 10/2/4ths 1/3 M.B. Bucks.	
	7		Visited S.S. Bedfs M.G. — All Battn. employ re instruction of Rifles machine guns.	
	18			

Lt Col ??? Cmdg
1/1 Bedf. I S Bn.

Army Form C. 2118.

WAR DIARY
or
INTELLIGENCE SUMMARY.

(Erase heading not required.)

Sept 1917

Place	Date	Hour	Summary of Events and Information	Remarks and references to Appendices
Estergade (Ell)	1917			
Fynsthere	3		Visited R.H. on courses out of line. Conference there with field gts.	
	6		Moved	
	8		Visited HQTS ii Corps. R.C.C. — Calais — Fd. R.C. &c	
	11		Conference of GOCs.	
	13		Visited Calais re found clerk &c.	
	20		18th Corps HQ & saw horse life &c.	
	21		— from 2 i.b. & RA re supervision of guns	
	23		HQTS 18th Corps	
Poperinghe	26		Moved Div HQ at Poperinghe	
	28		Took over line from HQTS ST. Div.	
	29		Visited Fd Brigades re refilling section — went to clothing & stores of RAMC 11 & 8 Divs.	
				CA.....Capt ....

89

MESSAGES AND SIGNALS.

This message is on a/c of:
28 Service.

TO: 18 Div A

Sender's Number: 78/44
Day of Month: 25
AAA

War Diary for Oct received

From: 18 Div A

Capt
DAAG

"A" Form
MESSAGES AND SIGNALS.

Army Form C. 2121
(In pads of 100)

TO: 18th Div A

Sender's Number: J 96
Day of Month: 24
In reply to Number: 78/43 A
AAA

Diary issue M please

[Stamp: HEAD QUARTERS 24 NOV 1917 DIVISION]
78/44 A

From
Place: Dadd
Time:

(Z) — Hughes Lond

WAR DIARY
or
INTELLIGENCE SUMMARY.
(Erase heading not required.)

Army Form C. 2118.

DA/DS/8/2
Vol 27

Place	Date	Hour	Summary of Events and Information	Remarks and references to Appendices
Top Ridge	15/17 Oct	2	Visited DADVS re... He civilly bore also explained situation to Staff Capt 19th.	
		3	RDVS	
			Col RA staff him all correspondence on hand	
		4	Pistol Artillery wired from Residents of Diversion birth & heard Boys detail — Same 3 men when leaving, as very carried out with all the truth — Interesting to watch 30% incident of Ambulance Stores at Bareilly on leaving the small trunk clothing manuring — Forty 15% of stone trunks to lumber — in care of D.A.V.S.	
		16	Moving to Hongh on Storough Road. DAVS at Bondencourt to see for administration	
		30	6 PM to see	
		17	1 AM to 11. DV	
		20	3 DV to 10 PM	
		24	Moved Office store to Potronnoffe	
		25	9 trucks of stores arrived at Kreiland which are now at Bondencourt — An instance of the uncertainty of road transport stores from Base.	
		26		
		31	2 no 14 bull dipt for reserve of restraction in ammunition	
				Colgrim Capt DDVS W.Div.

90

WAR DIARY
or
INTELLIGENCE SUMMARY.

Army Form C. 2118.

Place	Date	Hour	Summary of Events and Information	Remarks and references to Appendices
HERDINGHE	1917			91
	17		Returned from course at No 14. F.O. Dépôt	
	18		No. 4th off 41 X & cases.	
	19		5 h. guns of 114th overhauled	
	20		8 " " "	
	21		5 " " Yorkshire "	
			1 of A.A. section returned	
	22		Remainder of Bn. HQ moved to Elverdinghe Chateau.	
	23		5 h. guns of Norfolks overhauled	
	24		8 " " " ?	
	25		8 " " " Suffolks "	
			Wounded returned	

Morrison Capt
o/HAD 18 Dw.

WAR DIARY
or
INTELLIGENCE SUMMARY.
(Erase heading not required.)

Army Form C. 2118.

DAZS 182

10 of 29

92

Place	Date	Hour	Summary of Events and Information	Remarks and references to Appendices
RIVER DIMCRE	1917 Oct 11		Returned from leave	
			Visited HOOK'S lines	
	12		Moved to ROUSBRUGGE	
	27			
	15			
	22		Dismantled 16 L-guns of Bedfords.	
	23			
	28		Looks of Renier states that the site at 7 Louch no longer available - visited him S.E. in Hut 28 & 6 on H.12 a - saw 4 site there at A.12 a. 0.7 arranged with men Commanders - asked him for 4 nissen huts	
	30		Site his again	
	31		Who have informed request for nissen huts referred to HQRE for to at least two before going into new site -	
				M. Morran Lieut HQRE 10th Div

WAR DIARY or INTELLIGENCE SUMMARY

Army Form C. 2118.

BA905
18th Divn

Place	Date	Hour	Summary of Events and Information	Remarks and references to Appendices
Remains	1918 June	1	Visited site for new Divnl Staff as tk'd by XIX Corps. (Shul 28 M 4 & 5)	
			Incorporation in 4 Corps cont'd.	
Elverdinghe		3	Divn'l Arty about - hostile R.A. rec'd two re	
			S3 Inf: Bde attached (15 pm) rested Bde cancels in camps near Proven. War offrs - Lt.Col very short of horses -	
			Re Room enough to be nearer compld(?)	
		6	MOOS visits these a office.	
		8	Visited S3 Bde HQ, 73, Coy MGC	
		9	87 Bn HQ nr SAINT?. 1st Div	
		10	Started building Phimin hut for new camp at Elverdinghe Chateau. This was arranged by Colls through Sir Hugh are Cowell, who was detached to work Phimin through GHQ.	
		11	Visited Buffs.	
		12	SS Inf Bty - Mr Heak	
		13	MOOS visits these - Din at Elverdinghe Chateau	
		18	Bde moved to 53 Div.	
		19	Evan Pool Bryant moved in Lyons camp kept rebus'd??	
		21	Working.	
		24	Conference with MGGS & Gen or ?	
		25	Lrd MOOS to take advl. what thunds	
		28	Clearing church	
		29	Moved division a office. Div-Divnrn Hqrs moved Elverdinghe Cant OX4917 — 15846	

93

WAR DIARY / INTELLIGENCE SUMMARY

Army Form C. 2118.

Dargai
18th Divn.

VII 31

94

Place	Date	Hour	Summary of Events and Information	Remarks and references to Appendices
Hangu-Thal Road	19/6 Sept			
	1		May or marcho to H.Q. 1st army. Slept half day in lorry through between Systems.	
	2		Received tickets.	
	3		Supped an compartment in disturbance of Doubtha Suffolks stewds. 8 Royal Berks joined the Suffolks March returning stores lines TRIDENT to all concerned. Instructs Suffolks to have tent announce from Doubthas Suffolks to Sea Post.	
	4		Roads struck between even — Suffolks returned tents	
	5		Istanik — 5 Warragh — Sumo on halt.	
	6		Istanik —	
	7		Moves to Jalsuny — all personnel with Seltrage by rail. (self by road)	
February	8		Arrives Jalsuny — lorries arrived at noon. Remainder test plus cars from Burrie. Phote Rouen & Calais	
			as from 9:— Kotai host m Corps at Buppy Whys — Drew u Nfth army	
	11		Drew 12. 3" Mortars — Mortars & received 2:— Stores arrived from Base	
	12			
	13		Received stores from 12. Months on withdrawal. Sent these 3/b. guns & Shrapnel in Shot. to Sea Post.	

Place	Date	Hour	Summary of Events and Information	Remarks and references to Appendices
	17		Moved to Baboeuf - Visited HQ of the 3 Bns of br Rent. 18 Bdes - the former now SB Bde.	
	18		Visited Rearland at Achilly	
	20		20 Lorries for firewood of Rotors	
	23		13 tons at Rosthens - checked by HT.	
	26		3 Or Illyricum arrived as reinforcements	
	27		moved there stock open site knowns erented by 6 NCOs & S.Br.	
	28		Visited NCOs & Light Salvage officer at Tray. Coches have to be supplies to the 18 Batt Re. also to: Esterne extl HMT L18 Bde	

WAR DIARY
or
INTELLIGENCE SUMMARY.
(Erase heading not required.)

Army Form C. 2118.

Place	Date 19/8	Hour	Summary of Events and Information	Remarks and references to Appendices
Villequier aumont	Nov 4		To 18 Corps HQ. Warn visitor that there at F.A. 18th Corps doubts as delivery of what stores to him in collection by divisions or of Third Corps. Registered projector prisoners interested knowing that I have myself to arrange for him to inspect any battalion's rifles, all of them being in line so will see Bde at Cailloiel, who were first inspected by divl commander.	
	5		Shown on his dump, where all non-essential stores were to be sent. - (Bollard in Forest Rest. Received sundries transferred from HQ - many + stocks - which here sent to Base unit. - H. B. ' 105 - wrote for stores of H. B. ' 105 -	
	6			
	7			
	16			
	17		To Bde HQ. Questions on thank'na and But 13 Batt. + few stores of each - 2 R.70. Hardy on wheeler bridge +	
			6 pm - 2 motors overturned	
	19		7 guns + motors + returned to unit + one by lorry, guns received to behave on attack - Subsequently man	
	20		battle stations.	
	21		Battle started 4.0 a.m. - Lorries to be prepared to retire to green line - orders to retire to Beloncle received 10.30 am. At 5.45 pm had sent 2 lorries to Kit Store, however, but harassed other non-essential stores, supplies officer to self custody -	

96

War Diary or Intelligence Summary

Place: Villages-au-mont
Date: 1916

21/22
At 10.30 a.m. began loading up lorries for Bapaume — Clearing drunk by 2.30 a.m. — Then loaded 1500 suits I.B. clothing which had been used as a reserve for past carts — also S.B. Res. from this. Left on two lorries at 4.45 am for heavy to day. Where I & clothing & S.B. Res were left with S.mo officer The lorries to Bapaume arriving 6.30 am — at 10 am M.M. Hughes instructed me to demand 2½ stations & 8 hours 12, 6 newtons 70 Jenny & 2.5 pickers from Lent & lorries to time tack to Havernes, & Flavies to Lewis & 61 pickers — These were carried in tack at intervals by cars or to Bofilles & Pick. Bell on instructions from the Lieut. loving to Flesquieres — cleared clean clothing from thereof. 11 to Bath to Bapaume. Sent 3 lorries to hoping to Egypt. when the 1500 suits I.B. clothing & Nov lorries to Bapaume. Before sending on to hit there later. S.B. Res the were handed to San officer at Bapaume. At 11 hours returned & undent. — Sent 3 lorries to San Pont to draw some of the wire & any machine guns available. Remaining lorry to Railhead at Noyon to claim track retrieved — later was found to be impracticable in events & rendis bed tract of clean clothing from above — the laundry was cleaned & clothing but in tel store — At 4 am lorries to hickaning to reserve to Flecourt Send cyclist to Noyon to hasten return of lorry — this preriously sent liaised N.T. orderly up to let the lorries from going to Maulade but he was too late —

97

Army Form C. 2118.

WAR DIARY
or
INTELLIGENCE SUMMARY.
(Erase heading not required.)

98

Place	Date	Hour	Summary of Events and Information	Remarks and references to Appendices
Behrest	2nd 7a.		Reported to O.C. that no lorries were available. I was allotted two, to take ammunition to machine gun. Two lorry were standing on main thoroughfare road, but could not get all to Behrest in one trip — traffic could. 5.30 p.m. — lorries up gun re-ammunition lorry returned from Senon — loaded up & despatched both to Mericourt, the detachment going on foot. I remained with General Lander who had other lorries, which were found with Capt. Gibson practically cleared dump — Left at 7.30. Started a system to meet the 3 lorries returning from Senon, ran Rose round & direct them to Mericourt. Sandsack or Meripon — Rose revised from Sunpit but arrived 1.30 a.m. — found 3 lorries from Sunpit had arrived with [illegible]. Items + 8 Italians from — 7 British — set lorry with staff to [illegible] with orders to telephone M.T. Off. Mt. who no mentable to & Senon Sergeant — Then to go to Red Cross chris, knock, and to be recalled the stores — The lorry returned at 3 a.m. haning been unable to get through to Senon — meanwhile the 3 other lorries had been sent to Base to Base — Marshall — to clear truck there — at noon M.T Off. arrived, ordering not to go to & stores to Senon with all lorries & necessary to destroy hay which would not the removed — to whom & first lorry at 3 p.m. loaded up & proceed to M.T. & stores Red holding back, to distribute remainder of detachment on foot	
Mericourt	25			

Army Form C. 2118.

WAR DIARY or INTELLIGENCE SUMMARY.

99

Place	Date 1918	Hour	Summary of Events and Information	Remarks and references to Appendices
Thiersand/Arech	25		back of a car as this regiment was expected the himself - both our [illegible] had gone to Anthrea's District which this was regarded their such remained to Brens. I arranged to hunt their mail/Rackhays - The 3 lorries returned at 5.30 p.m. fully loaded with blankets, bivy etc + spare lorries - Blankets the lorries with the men voluntarily. Their Coys (now) regiment, having arranged with Col Marks O.C. 3rd Bde. I.T. that, in case of need, he would issue order to their detachment - In this mission some of the loading slews in the lorries has to be [illegible] to Essex [illegible] for duties which he regard regulations of the greatest importance - fell at 7.30 p.m.	
[illegible] Benard			Arrived 12.30 a.m. - had to clear [illegible] there from [illegible]. pushes of blankets to Base + to M.T. work. Rather at 5.30 a.m. Received an order that is is to be [illegible] convenient to this escort to march to + hand [illegible] at once. In [illegible] shops and the order, but knowing not [illegible] Brigades would be, I decided to proceed there - both a car, this would have been [illegible] + as totals subsequently showed, the removal of all my lorries + personnel was at least as regards 2 lorries, [illegible] of [illegible] - Left there at 5.30 a.m.	

100

Place	Date 1918	Hour	Summary of Events and Information	Remarks and references to Appendices
Audigneul	Mch 27		Roused 2.30 a.m. at 9 am returned all remaining vehicles. Unable, in spite of its decoration also some J.B. He to much - saw Staff Capt K-a.b. then immediate regiment - HH.(M.G) interview (heard nothing) rifle fire on our front. Shots the nothing (no reed) but this should not be do. After only 1 could meaning - Shaw did not carry out orders - Ruthert told to fire & throw returned there at 11.30 km arrive 6.30 km Intention should send stores up by lorry as rather available - but had uncertain, but the baths Compiegne not three at Rosieres (Somme)	
Marie Bruno	28		Ettre - again quietly harrassed by lack of car - decided to truck on board with 15 Rn ruck lorry provided to General the Ambulance, when a truck was badly cleared & stores also taken from a truck for Off 2nd S.& Cavalry to Breveton which was not being cleared - Sent lorry with stores to Longueneau T tonnage by Rev. Howard to Ho.Offich - asked for a car to be allotted to me - Proceeding to Breveton - Rev Howard returned, with message that motherful of car was untrouble -	
Breveton	29		Left Compiegne which was bucked - Could drive could arrive of Sally Ruen at 10.30 km Mr Irmine Tried to arrange as any	

WAR DIARY
or
INTELLIGENCE SUMMARY.

Army Form C. 2118.

(Erase heading not required.)

Place	Date	Hour	Summary of Events and Information	Remarks and references to Appendices
Couhéque	29		The 10th Sikh Section had patrol was obtained of which forces infantry in right abandoned. Left at 5.30 P.M. but started by escort message from HQ. 111 Corps with instructions to proceed from Couhéque by Lewis's 20 Tickler guns. Could only take lorry load & then proceeded to Wiéconst — Picked S. of Staincuis — this destination was obtained from 2nd 7 Coy.	
Wiéconst	30		Arrived 3 a.m. — 2nd Lieut. of D.H.Q. had arrived section of M.T. Coy found one D.H.Q. to use up their lorries. Proceeded due forward there is not reconcile tent's lorries to offer Couhéque to collect remainder of machine guns came after dark.	
Staincher	31		It is stated for administration — lorries H.Q. at Staincher. Noted M.T.S. — Instructed res. to there as retable that was another would arrive last night. Two lorries broke down so kept away — Div states that no one in D.K. available. H.Q. Coy kindly provided water — send M.C. corporal to the lorries & so was able to come by south the arterial road to Baithins for Dir. still Couhéqne the 15th. Therefore moved	

W. Moore
O/C H.Q. 15 Div.

WAR DIARY or INTELLIGENCE SUMMARY

Army Form C. 2118.

WA DOE/8/7
J.A. 33

102

Place	Date	Hour	Summary of Events and Information	Remarks and references to Appendices
H Jaffa	1918 July 1		Two horses recovered - small quantities of tea of arms little of arms from Corps - who has drawn from Sup. Pk. & stores of same inside Impossible to try other means of supply - Lorry had to be taken daily to Richleas. The location of Buthen's any unreliable but Corps ordered trying friendly humans pattern - hostile all with Lorry, hostiles to obtain stones from other provisions. There was want of any salvage pattern. No establish time hostiles. 2nd of B.W. Shot at Yerville emerged with 600 yds slightly off ahead shore, but flammable at 15 the & return. Lurd turned to know they had when observed 10,000 but looked' weak their retirement from the river Louvain. attitude.	
	3		To Jaffa by train - Reached Samina - Lent time along in Lorry Jaffa from saving. Horse shore, but experienced - D.W.F.	
	4		Move to Salem - as have convened for division - D.W.F. at Corps	
Salem	5			
	6		Received instructions from XXII Corps to advance to remove 40 M/s - 5. 20 - 50 - M. Enemy Reserve had followed up the situation - 8 by own OUDJ. Advanced to S.B. brit. Line so 116	

Army Form C. 2118.

WAR DIARY
or
INTELLIGENCE SUMMARY.
(Erase heading not required.)

103

Place	Date	Hour	Summary of Events and Information	Remarks and references to Appendices
Salbris	4/11/18 7		Found F.B. O.R. were returned by D.A.D.O.S. [illegible] again would be O.H.O.G.S. Saw night - Capts. [illegible] I went up the trench to they were out. Inspected two Coys D.A. [illegible] in winter. Home - there is to the latter unable to fight back - having no there equipment or [illegible] & 15 A.M. & 4 new Pack we then moved have been [illegible] roads - also C.R.S. Humey had two or 3 [illegible] all without travels with light cant - stores have been distributed by S.J. This is not satisfactory. There is not be rationed by this [illegible] attention these has been [illegible] etc. Men shoes, I.B.R.S. [illegible] flannels, boots, etc. & clothing - [illegible] Matters.	
	9			
	10		Reported that O/C [illegible] to attend [illegible] for round the infantry.	
	11		During both intervals received - no replies [illegible] on [illegible] Park - [illegible] F.T. [illegible] understood from [illegible] could not arrange for refills of [illegible] to run O.O. [illegible] moved from [illegible] Battalion all our of time to-night. 15 Bn. to Overton.	
	13		Their numbers are ill.	
	14			
	15		Kantor 15 Battn. [illegible]	

WAR DIARY or INTELLIGENCE SUMMARY

Army Form C. 2118.

Place	Date	Hour	Summary of Events and Information	Remarks and references to Appendices
Tilloux	Aug 10		To Bde. Staff Capt not there - called at my office	
	11		Visited To Bde Staff Capt & all officers at Bn H.Q. Received some photos - maps from officials	
	13		Spent emb. received	
	18		Inspection of Rifles & fuses of re-crts. Spent emb.	
	19		Service to Sandpit at Pont Remy for fuses inspection. Rifles have to continue work to Sealy so I... tail end of H.Q. No firing from Bare	
	20		Spent Rude detail stores received	
	21		No stories	
	22		Visited Rucheux - hilly but Sommes - Workshops 22/8/18 at Regnisy - Sandpit at Pont Remy - To Fourth H.Q. Carillon	
	25		Spent emb. returned to Bare	
	26		To Carillon - no stores there	
Carillon	27		Moves to Carillon	
	29		Stores to S3 W.O. Ian urged to continue to accumulate	
	30		Rifles found very well otherwise all correct	

Army Form C. 2118.

WAR DIARY
or
INTELLIGENCE SUMMARY.
(Erase heading not required.)

DAQG 18th Divn
May 1918

Vol 33 B

105

Place	Date 1918	Hour	Summary of Events and Information	Remarks and references to Appendices
Corbellen	May 1		Wires to SS Wile at Beaucourt. Div & Wilkie	
			14 Wires from Heavy & Divs	
	2		Wires to Sir Boyle	
	5		Off to Barleaveal	
	6		2 Br (heav) at represent + on 6 Wires Boupe Solicits possible site near Dernville. Saw O.M.G. M Corks why bad to move at Beaucourt, the site not being in Divl area. Apphys on Tilloloy told him so far forward Inf(Lys) brigade	
	7		2 Talkinstar to Sr brev - arrange site there	
	8		Completes move from Cordillon	
	9		Wires to Sup brigades RA + lorries returning with Salvage	
	10		2 Railhead Pombauville will lorries that wh stores then a returns out to Railhead formts - left M'head & arrang job bought to him	
	11		To two Wires on Boots as to troop kets	
	12		Move there	
	13		Inf on various questions - hold all Salvage Dumps - S3	
			bit re	
	22		New T.S.T. hing to complete to tank E. asked J to put me in the mushroom as to retention of these brendeis came -	

Army Form C. 2118.

WAR DIARY
or
INTELLIGENCE SUMMARY.
(Erase heading not required.)

106

Place	Date	Hour	Summary of Events and Information	Remarks and references to Appendices
In the line nr Jam	May 22 1918		2.2. Bedfords relieved both Own Battns - saw C.O. re reinforcements &	
	28		4/4 fins allotted to Brigade	
	31		4 " " " " to 5th of who for Reinforcement camp. Recall of stores now issued & units all now well delivered —	

Morrow Lt Col
DAQMG

107

WAR DIARY
or
INTELLIGENCE SUMMARY.

Army Form C. 2118.

NANOS 18 Bn
fol 35

Place	Date 1918	Hour	Summary of Events and Information	Remarks and references to Appendices
Inthings nr Bois J.	June 1		Moved to site vacated by Fd Amb. Clothes to Pare.	
	6		On leave	
	28		Brades by heavy planes. A/Sgt Jones NCO A/Sgt Allen & McKirk killed	
	29		Bomb there two R.E.8 at Monticeray	
	30		To B.H.Q. at Conteay	
	3/7/18			

Morrison Major
o/c 1st 18 Bn

18th Division "A"

Herewith War Diary
for month of July.
Delay regretted.

Thomson
Major
D.A.D.O.S. 18 Di

16/8/18

forward
JH

"A" Form
MESSAGES AND SIGNALS.

Army Form C. 2121
(In pads of 100.)

TO — DADOS Signals
~~BGSA~~ ROHA

Sender's Number.	Day of Month.	In reply to Number.	AAA
R 990	15		

Hasten War Diary for July due 10th inst

mr Harrell

what about it?
no duplicate in cover —
15/8
CRE

From 18 Div A

Whipps Capt

WAR DIARY or INTELLIGENCE SUMMARY

Army Form C. 2118.

DADS 187 WL 36

108

Place	Date	Hour	Summary of Events and Information	Remarks and references to Appendices
Mailleul in Bois	July 1 1918		General Routine work	
	2		Visited MDTS & 60 in Corps Trenches —	
	3		General Routine work —	
	4		ditto	
	5		Visited tried thawing engine when the ko'd OWTS with MDTS	
	6		General Routine work	
	7/8		To Carillon and Aldershot MDDS. — Visited ADMS 147 there.	
	9		General Routine work	
	10		Lieut Wt. Brakest wound to Units — MDTS visited	
	11		General Routine work	
	12		Moved to Cul Obn	
Cul Obn	13		Arranged for installation of prisoners - Refills & Intellisons of Luris food in which is made fr th in den	
	14			
	15		Visited 53 Bde MDS - W.W.W Rent. - Reddition Caual - Bet Pall	
	16		in its MDS Corko -	
	17		Visits HQ of 3 Ind. Brigades —	
	18		Ambulance Commanders Present for instruction	
	19		General Routine work	
	20		Visited 55 Bde MDS - Previous - Baths etc Lavories	

109

WAR DIARY
or
INTELLIGENCE SUMMARY.

Army Form C. 2118.

Place	Date	Hour	Summary of Events and Information	Remarks and references to Appendices
Willows July 27	1918 27/28		General Routine work	
	28		General Routine work	
			To 111 Corps to relieve MOTT who to go on leave on 30/7/18 when British weekly at DHQ	
	31		Moved to A. Mootein	

Moorman Major

WAR DIARY or INTELLIGENCE SUMMARY.

Army Form C. 2118.

DADS 182 / JA 37

110

Place	Date 1918	Hour	Summary of Events and Information	Remarks and references to Appendices
Corbay	Aug 18		General Routine	
	19		Touring Reconnoitring Several battle stores - no car available.	
	20		No car available - General Routine	
	21		To Heavy Mobile Workshop Dept S. at Rouxline for his Ryes - borrowed car from Train Off - Light Railway Officer called re Stores for Grenville - Received ford van	
	22		General Routine	
	23		General Routine	
	24		General Routine	
	25		Moved to Warloy - attended Conference w/ D.	
Warloy	26		Moved to Richmond - wrote re Reinforcements - Wrote Buckland	
Richmond	27		Wired front it on Daddy wagons - Wrote Buckland - no refilling. Consequently no Delivery of Trd Store - Wrote Browning with Remarks.	
	28		Moved transport back in readiness of transfer from Warloy.	
	29		Lost S called. 2 Buckland (Capwell) - also off with LLD - borrowed car from Tram Off to take L. Gun Montgene our view to 52 Bde.	
	30		General Routine	
	31		To Park for Lorries mountings - Wanted car	

Morrison Major
BMOS 18 Dn.

Army Form C. 2118.

WAR DIARY
or
INTELLIGENCE SUMMARY.
(Erase heading not required.)

Instructions regarding War Diaries and Intelligence Summaries are contained in F. S. Regs. Part II and the Staff Manual respectively. Title pages will be prepared in manuscript.

Place	Date 1918	Hour	Summary of Events and Information	Remarks and references to Appendices
Watten	Aug 1		Arranging new hunts re field Bakery etc: at HATS - main workrooms at Corps siding at HATS	
	2		General Routine work	
	3		do	
	4		Attended Improvement.	
	5		General Routine work. 8 Ovens Reached?	
	6		General Routine work & lorries to San Pick and one to Abbeville	
	7		To Abbeville re Hospital stores	
	8		Two lorries to San Pick - 4 lorries at Rickhard	
	9		Visited by HAT 2 - two lorries to San Pick	
	10		7½ tons at Rickhard - 6 lorries & tents lorries Corps Reserve gold clothing - new tents	
	11		from Rickhard afternoon.	
	12		General Routine	
Lambres	12		Moves to Lambres.	
	13		General Routine	
	14		Head Bakers went on leave though been returned from Corps.	
	15		Visited Adapt board at IRF - general nature	
	16		Arrange arrangements necessary for running of Rly Bakery Doullens.	
	17		2 Field ovens 1 box) re new Side re end of advance - Albert I - arranged with RAF Ballon section as to Frévent	II

Army Form C. 2118.

WAR DIARY
or
INTELLIGENCE SUMMARY.
(Erase heading not required.)

Instructions regarding War Diaries and Intelligence Summaries are contained in F.S. Regs., Part II. and the Staff Manual respectively. Title pages will be prepared in manuscript.

DADVS 18 H Co
IOf 39

16/10/18

112

Place	Date 16/18	Hour	Summary of Events and Information	Remarks and references to Appendices
Pitcaird Sept 1			General Routine work	
Vineuil	2		Moved to Vineuil	
	3		Moved to Catachelis Valley	
	4		Released R.R. students	
	5		Visited 3 Inf. Bde HQ	
	6		" S'3 Bde.	
	7		" New Railhead Station	
	8		Turn Park inspection Pack Bde p/c	
	9		General Routine work	
	10		ADVS called	
	11/12		General Routine work	
			Visits new area - Seleuth Sta - met DDVS, visited 18 Res	
	14		Returns on vaccination parades of g battalions	
	15		Moved to Merka area	
Merka	16		Railhead - arranging for arr of Dornerille	
	17		General Routine work	
	18		ADVS called	
	19		Visited DADVS 74 Div. in new scheme of bulk + detail rations of	
	20		ustails	

113

Place	Date 1918	Hour	Summary of Events and Information	Remarks and references to Appendices
Muende Selby	21		Reliefs as per circle 1 A.D.V.S. re Establishment	
	22		General Routine work	
	23		Further Reliefs Horses to BB. iii. C.T. off. Fourth M.T. No.1	
	24		General Routine work	
	25		Moves to Courelles	
Courelles	26		General Routine work	
	27		Moves to ots 1 to rear Murdu - Reserve Section	
Murdu	28			
	29		General Routine work	
	30			

CMordaim Major
ADVS 1s Div.

78 Div. A.   Secret

Herewith war
diary for Oct.

C.A. Morrison
Major
8/11/18   AA&QMG

["A" BRANCH,
HEADQUARTERS,
78th DIVISION.
No. 7858
Date 9-11-18]

instant and onwards.
Revised orders are bei[ng]
Reception Camps.

3. BRIDGES.

One of two Bridges on
Central is being closed

27th Octr. 1918.

D.A.D.O.S., 18TH DIVISION.
No.
Date 28th

Army Form C. 2118.

WAR DIARY
or
INTELLIGENCE SUMMARY.
(Erase heading not required.)

DADOS 18th Divn
Art 42

116

Place	Date	Hour	Summary of Events and Information	Remarks and references to Appendices
Huda	Oct 1		Preparing orders to 1.2 v 18 DAs. 13th Corps HQs re receiving them.	
	2		Reconn HQs informs - moved 12 DA & others to Div.	
			moved to Beauval	
	3		On leave to Paris	
	12		Returned from Paris.	
			moved 18 DA & others to HAFL 13th Corps	
			General Routine work	
	13		moved to Forvestry level	
	14			
	16		moved to Moreuil	
	19		moved to the Adrien	
	24			
	27		General Routine work	
	31			Morcourt Indre
				1 MMG 18 Div

HEAD QUARTERS
9 NOV 1918
18TH DIVISION

WAR DIARY
or
INTELLIGENCE SUMMARY.

(Erase heading not required.)

Army Form C. 2118.

Place	Date	Hour	Summary of Events and Information	Remarks and references to Appendices
Le Cateau	1918 Nov 1		General Routine work	
	2		Found difficulty in getting up supplies owing to moves on line — considerable difficulty in keeping in touch with Brigade — finally arranged to have a Lorry	
	3			
	4		touch with Brigade	
	5		tasks of Brigade	
	6		General Routine work	
	7			
	8		Divisions came out of line	
	9		General Routine work	
	10			
	11		Armistice	
	12		Moved to Sevrin	
	13			
	14/15		General Routine work	
	16		on leave to Paris	

114

DADTS/8/2 Army Form C. 2118.

115

WAR DIARY
or
INTELLIGENCE SUMMARY.
(Erase heading not required.)

Place	Date 1918	Hour	Summary of Events and Information	Remarks and references to Appendices
Iurian Lipny	Dec 1		On leave	
	20		Returned from leave	
	21		Visited BADTS/VIII Echelon Cavalry	
	22		Lorries arrived from Hours by road. Lorries T.4. had been used to bring drivers under lorry arrangements owing to shortage of trucks.	
	23		General Routine work	
	24		x mas day	
	25		Visited Officers to whigus him whilst on leave	
	26		General Routine work	
	27			
	28			
	29			
	30		General Routine work	
	31			

Morrison Major
DADOS 18 Div

1800 A

Herewith War Diary for month
of Feb 1919.
Please acknowledge receipt

28.2.19

[signature]
BROSTROM

Army Form C. 2118.

WAR DIARY
INTELLIGENCE SUMMARY.
(Erase heading not required.)

Instructions regarding War Diaries and Intelligence Summaries are contained in F. S. Regs., Part II. and the Staff Manual respectively. Title pages will be prepared in manuscript.

DADTS 182 / Vol 4 43 / 117

Place	Date 1919	Hour	Summary of Events and Information	Remarks and references to Appendices
LIGNY	Feb 1.		(TRANSFER Vol 4.4)	
	2		145 Y annual inspection before departure to France	
	3		34 Y H.Q. annual inspection before departure to Base	
	6		78 H.D. Y annual inspection before departure to France	
	7		Capt. SS TELBART relinquishes from duties to Englesbrecht	
	8		10 CZ annual return passed. Marched for sale	
			75 CZ annual inspection - Seyfermon	
	9		Capt. Pt WILLIAMS RAMC to CG'S mis - Seyfermon	
			Inspector Keating CZ annual parade.	
	10		170 CZ annual return with lectures at MARETZ army mis 715 A	
	13		30 MVS head to CAMBRAI under H DDVS 3rd Army	
	14		DADVS return from Kin help Have setting for ADVS	
	15		attended meeting at SOLESMES + LECATEAU	
	17		rode 30 MVS at CAMBRAI	

Army Form C. 2118.

WAR DIARY
or
INTELLIGENCE SUMMARY.
(Erase heading not required.)

Instructions regarding War Diaries and Intelligence Summaries are contained in F. S. Regs., Part II. and the Staff Manual respectively. Title pages will be prepared in manuscript.

Place	Date 1918	Hour	Summary of Events and Information	Remarks and references to Appendices
LIGNY	Feb 18		Motor Cz arrive from re Valentin	
	19		Motor Cz arrive from re S.Cour	
	20		Motor see & 1/17 Cz arrive at WALINCOURT. Army HQrs private 273 Fld Amce moving into 6 Fd Cof a HQrs	
	22		Arrived SAH & 1/20 Cz arrive at MARETZ	
	23		Arrived SAH & 1/20 Cz arrive at MARETZ DADR.	
			Inspecting 15 Amces etc DADR.	
	24		Major G. WILLIAMSON and 6 others left for BOOS 15 Feb	
			Arrived new at WALINCOURT vice Major Williamson	
	27		Reports Cz arrived for inspection £ ABBEVILLE & also for motor	
	28		Major G. WILLIAMSON returned £ on leave 15th February from home L. M. VERNEY Capt. in charge of Records N Cof a ADS	

Buckingham
DADMS

118
END

www.ingramcontent.com/pod-product-compliance
Lightning Source LLC
Chambersburg PA
CBHW081427160426
43193CB00013B/2212